Government & Ministry in the Local Church

Government & Ministry in the Local Church

Stephen Kaung

Christian Fellowship Publishers, Inc.
New York

Copyright © 2018
Christian Fellowship Publishers, Inc.
New York
All Rights Reserved.

ISBN: 978-1-68062-131-0
eBook ISBN: 978-1-68062-675-9

Available from the Publishers at:

11515 Allecingie Parkway
Richmond, Virginia 23235
www.c-f-p.com

Printed in the United States of America

Preface

The church of God has its universal and local aspects. When we think of its government, we naturally think of its local aspect. Christ himself alone is the Head of the body, but He puts the elders in authority. The elders of the church stand for its government; they represent the authority of Christ. However, they are not the authority of the church. They serve as the neck, not the Head. They are not to rule over the church themselves. As the neck, they must present all the feeling of the body to the Head, and the wishes of the Head to the body. They serve as the go-between. To remain a neck, and never become a head, elders must always be plural in number.

These elders are chosen because they show more spiritual maturity and responsibility in the church. They must serve spiritually and diligently. Strict discipline and deep dealings are required to not rule over others, but allow Christ to be the Head of the church. Blessed is the church that has faithful elders!

Government and ministry are both essential in the building up of the local church. While local government manifests the *headship* of Christ, the local ministry of the word builds up the *life* of Christ in His body. Just as the apostle Paul said to the elders of Ephesus, "And now I commit you to God, and to the word of his grace, which is able to build you up and give to you an inheritance among all the sanctified" (Acts 20:32).

Contents

Preface...5
Note 8

Part One: The Government **11**
1—The Church: Universal and Local.................................13
2—The Necessity of Government in the Local Church..........19
3—The Development of Local Church Government 27

Part Two: Elders..**41**
4— Delegated Authority 43
5—The Plurality of Elders..51
6—The Nature of Eldership 55
7—How to Exercise Oversight 61
8—The Qualifications of Elders...65
9—How Elders are Chosen 71
10—The Saints and Elders 73
11—Elders in the Time of Recovery 77

Part Three: The Ministry of the Word...................................**87**
12—Body Ministry 89
13—The Ministry of God's Word...93
14—The Ministers of the Word...97
15—Local Ministry of the Word..107
16—How Local Ministry Develops......................................115
17—Our Need for Local Ministry.......................................123

Part Four: The Minister of the Word.................................**133**
18—The Minister's Attitude 135
19—The Minister is in the Ministry 141
20—Necessities for Ministry 151

Note

In June 1991, at the Christian Family Conference in Richmond Virginia, special leadership training sessions were held as an optional time over the theme Government and Ministry in the Local Church. Attendees were required to read II Corinthians, I and II Timothy and Titus five times beforehand as well as the books *The Ministry of God's Word* and *Rethinking the Work**, both by Watchman Nee.

Unless otherwise indicated,
Scripture quotations are from the
New Translation by J. N. Darby

---

* This book is currently volume II of *The Church and the Work*. It has also been called *Concerning Our Missions* and *The Normal Christian Church Life*.

Introduction

John 3:12—If I have said the earthly things to you, and ye believe not, how, if I say the heavenly things to you, will ye believe?

Before we begin, I would like to say a few words to clarify what we call training sessions. Only our Lord Jesus can train us. The Holy Spirit is the only trainer, and we are all trainees. I'm not qualified to train anybody. I'm still under training. So do not look at me but look at the Lord Jesus, and together we look to Him that He may train us to make us what He wants us to be, that we may be useful to Him.

We will focus our attention on the government and the ministry of local assemblies. We are not just dealing with spiritual principles but with the practice of spiritual truth. We like to talk about spiritual principles because these lift us up to the third heaven, and we enjoy them. But naturally, we do not like to talk about practice. When you talk about practice, it seems that we are pulled down to earth and must face problems and realities. That's the reason why everybody likes the letter to the Ephesians, and nobody really likes the Corinthian letters. But thank God that He is not only spiritual, but His spirituality is practical. He gives us letters to the Ephesians and Corinthians.

Someone just asked me before these training sessions, "Why is it that this time you talk about the local church and the government and ministry of the local church? You dropped down from the third heaven! It is a letdown." In previous years for the main conference themes, we spoke on *The King is Coming* and *The Kingdom of God*.* Now I would ask you, How can the kingdom come? How can the King return if the bride is not ready? It is the church that is holding back His return because the church has not been built; the bride has not made herself ready. We cannot be too spiritual and not practical. We have to get into the practical side to see the spiritual side being fulfilled.

---

* During the Christian Family Conference (1991) there continued to be a main theme, similar to the previous years, with a focus on God's Eternal Purpose—the spiritual principles. Other speakers took up that theme while Stephen Kaung held these special training sessions.

Part One: The Government

1—The Church: Universal and Local

Matthew 16:17—I will build my assembly [church], and hades' gates shall not prevail against it.

Before we look into government and ministry in the local church setting, we need to begin with a basic understanding of what a local church truly is.

There is one church. We will call it the church universal. Even though the term universal is not in the Scripture, it does describe it correctly. There is one church in the universe; it is the church universal. Everyone who believes in the Lord Jesus, who is born again, who has been redeemed by the precious blood, who belongs to the Lord, is in that church. From the first one who believed in the Lord in the first century to the last one who will believe in the Lord—all are in this one church universal. It spans over 2000 years, and it covers every corner of this earth. This is the complete church of God. This is the church to which you and I belong. Our Lord Jesus in Matthew 16:18 said, "On this rock I will build My church and the gates of Hades shall not prevail against it." *On this rock*, that is himself—He is the Rock. *I will build My church*—this is the church universal. *The gates of Hades shall not prevail against it.*

But at the same time as having the church universal, you also have the church local. In Matthew 18:20, the Lord said, "Where two or three are gathered together unto My name [in any place] there am I in the midst of them." *Where*—is locality; *two or three*—is plurality; *gathered together*, or assembled together, *unto My name*, the name of the Lord Jesus, that is, where two or three put themselves under the authority of Christ, the Lord said, *I am there in their midst*—this is the church. And this church is the church local.

Again, we do not have the word local in the Scriptures, but it describes it well. The Lord said, "if your brother sins against you." Most likely, the brother who sins against you is with you. If he is thousands of miles away, I think it will be very difficult for him to sin against you. That's the reason why we love our brothers who are thousands of miles away. If two or three or more who live in the same locality know each other, they rub against each other, they meet together, they serve the Lord together, there are plenty of opportunities of one sinning against the other because we are still in the flesh. So, it cannot refer to the church universal; it refers to the church local because wherever brothers and sisters live, they rub against each other, step on each other, and sin against each other.

If your brother sins against you, what will you do? According to the law, it's "an eye for an eye, a tooth

1—The Church: Universal and Local

for a tooth." But that's the law, and you are not under the law you are under grace. How will you react under grace when your brother or your sister sins against you? Well, you may say, "Unfortunately we are brothers and sisters, we are believers, and I have to forgive you because that is the command of the Lord. And I have to forgive you from my heart. If I do not forgive you from my heart, the Lord knows my heart, and He will hold me to it." So you say, "Okay, I'll forgive you." But is that all? Is that grace? No, that is not enough. If your brother sins against you, and you have forgiven him, you then begin to think of your brother and not just of yourself. He has sinned against you. He may have sinned against you without really knowing it. Sometimes he may know it, but sometimes he may not know it; and because of this, he will suffer before the Lord. You love your brother, and you don't want him to suffer. So you go and tell him what he has done. This is not to put him down or to vindicate yourself, but you are trying to restore your brother in love.

If your brother does not listen to you, your duty is not finished yet. Your love for your brother is such that you have to find another brother or two whom that one will respect. Then you all go to him again and try to restore him. If he still does not listen to you, what do you do? You tell the church. Now you cannot tell the church universal because it's too big. It is so big that you cannot touch it. So evidently, when our

Lord said to tell the church, this must be the church local. It must be the church where you are, where you brethren are gathering together. There is the church local (18:15-20).

In the church local you have many problems. Problems will come up and thank God problems will be solved. By solving these problems, the life of the church grows. That is the church local.

We must not think that since there is the church universal and there is the church local, therefore there are two churches. No, there is only one church. The church local is the local expression or the manifestation of the church universal. Why? It is for practical reasons. We are still in the flesh. One day when we put on the resurrection body, a spiritual body, then the church local disappears. But today we are still in this mortal body; and being in this flesh we are limited. We are limited by time and by space. By time—if we live today we do not live in the first century. By space—if you are now in Richmond you are no longer in Sydney, Australia. We are limited because we are still in this mortal body. For practical reasons, you have to be gathered together with those who are with you at the same time in the same place. Otherwise, how are you going to meet with them?

The church local is to put the spiritual principles of the church universal into practice. The church local is not another church from the church universal. It is not as if the church universal is concerned only with

1—The Church: Universal and Local

spiritual principles, and it is somewhere in heaven, never coming down upon this earth. Some people would probably like it that way. It is not that the church local is God's people coming together, organized into a kind of religious club without any spiritual principles being put into practice but instead practicing what they think is right. These are wrong concepts of the church.

There is only one church. The church universal gives us the spiritual principles, but the church local is to put these principles into practice. The church universal is the ultimate goal, the church local is the process.

How does God build the church universal? He builds it by building the church local. From the very beginning of the book of Acts to the very end we see Him building local churches. It begins with the building up of the church in Jerusalem, and it ends up with the church in Rome. It is by the building of the church local that the church universal is finally built. Otherwise, the church will never be built.

In Revelation 2-3 the seven churches in Asia Minor are described as the seven golden lampstands. These are the instruments for the testimony of Jesus in seven different localities in Asia Minor. The risen Lord as the High Priest, as the Lord over His house, is walking among the seven golden lampstands. He is examining them, trimming them, supplying them and building them up. But when you come to Revelation

21-22 you see the holy city, the New Jerusalem. If you can picture it, the New Jerusalem is actually one giant lampstand. The foundation is the base of that lampstand, and the wall is built upon that base. At the top, there is the throne of God and of the Lamb. The light of that lampstand is the Lamb himself. The New Jerusalem is a giant lampstand.

How does this New Jerusalem come into being? How is it built? When is it built? Where is it built? It is by building the seven churches in Asia Minor, and by building all the local churches throughout the centuries. At the very end, after all of the building work with the local churches is complete, the church universal appears. Then you no longer find the church local because the work is done.

What is the work of God? Our Lord Jesus said, "My Father worketh hitherto and I work" (John 5:17). What is the work of the Father? What is the work that our Lord Jesus did while He was on earth? What is the work that the Holy Spirit is doing today? God has one work, and that one work is building the church. The church is the body of Christ and will be the bride of the Lamb. God loves His Son. He said, "It is not good for Him to be alone." He wants to give Him a helpmate, a counterpart. And that is the work of the Father. That is the work of the Son. That is the work of the Holy Spirit. He is preparing the bride for His beloved Son

2 — The Necessity of Government in the Local Church

Isaiah 9:6c — and the government shall be upon his shoulder…

Why do we need government? The whole Bible talks about government. Our God is the Creator of all. He governs this universe. His dominion is over everything. He sets up His government in this universe. This includes not only the universe that you can see but also the universe that is unseen. He is God and He rules over all.

God also has His government in the church. Christ is the head of the church which is His body. The government is upon His shoulders. In the church, we need to recognize Christ as the head. He is our government. He is the ruler, the king. He is our authority.

Government in the Body of Christ

It is essential for us to hold fast the head as it says in Colossians 2:19: "holding fast the head, from whom all the body, ministered to and united [or gathered] together by the joints and bands, increases with the increase of God." How can the church be built? How can the body increase with the increase of God? Hold fast the head. When you think of the head you think of government because it is the head that governs the body.

Do we hold fast the head? This speaks to every member of the body. Every member of the body must hold fast the head. Do we allow His government to come upon us? In our personal lives, do we let Him be our head? Has there come a time in your life that you surrendered yourself to Him and took Him as your Lord as your King, as your Government? Have you told the Lord that from now on He is your Master, you will obey Him in all things? Have you done that? Do you do that every day? Do you renew your consecration every day? Hold fast to the head.

In all our daily spiritual life there is a constant struggle within us or around us over who is going to be the head. All the temptations that come upon us tempt us not to hold fast Christ as our head. How we need to be watchful and pray that daily, moment by moment, we hold fast Christ as the head.

If we all hold fast Christ as the head the Scripture says all the body will be united together. The reason why the body is divided is that we are not holding fast the head. Someone is not holding fast the head, or no one is holding fast the head. And that's the problem. If we all in our daily life hold fast Christ as the head, then the government is upon His shoulder and not

2—The Necessity of Government in the Local Church

upon our shoulders. Then all the body will automatically be united together.

The result is not only to be united together, but to be ministering one to another by joints of supply and bands of connection; and we will increase with the increase of God. This is spiritual principle applied. We must hold fast the head.

In the church, there is no other head but Christ. We are not for Paul, we are not for Apollos, we are not for Cephas, we are all for Christ*. Today, the reason divisions in the church happen is we remove Christ as the head and replace Him with something else. It can be a spiritual person, a spiritual giant, a teaching, a doctrine, a system, a form, a tradition, etc. Whenever we do not hold fast Christ as the head the body disintegrates. So, first of all, we have to hold fast Christ as the head.

Christ is the head of every man, and that word man includes women also†. He is the head of every man, everyone, every believer. Do not ask why the church is not built. Do not ask why we are not united. Do not ask why we do not see the body functioning. Just ask one questions: Do I hold fast Christ as the head?

The head is where the government is. It is where the wisdom is, where the control is, where the will is;

---

* See I Corinthians 1:11-13; 3:3-5
† I Corinthians 11:3

but under the head, you have the body. The head needs a body. It needs a body to express itself. And the church is His body. What is a body? A body is a living organism. It is not a dead organization, and it is a living organism full of life. Since there is life there is order.

Is there any organization in the church local? Yes, but that organization is not something you organize from the outside, it is organized by the life within. Look at your body, it is a perfect organization. Everything is perfectly organized. No one organ is in the wrong place. Now suppose some organ of the body is in the wrong place, you know what will happen. But in a normal body all the body parts are perfectly united together, fitted together; and so, each part of the body ministers one to another. There is a divine order there. And that divine order is according to divine life. The organization comes from the life of the organism.

And if I may I will use that illustration a little further to show something more on the government in the local church. What is the connection between the body and the head? What part of the body connects the head? The neck. All the nerve systems go through the neck. All the impulses that you receive from the members of the body go through the neck to the head. And all the commands and responses come from the head through the neck to the different members of the body. I would like to use this as an illustration, though it is not a perfect illustration.

2—The Necessity of Government in the Local Church

Christ is the head. He never removes himself from being the head of the church. He is not only the head of the church universal but the church local too. Do not think that in the church local He is no longer the head, He is still the head but for practical reasons, the way He governs His body as a local assembly is to set up a "neck" there. And the neck is the eldership that you find in the Scripture. That's the government. The neck is the passage or the connection between the head and the other parts of the body. The neck is not the commanding post. The commanding post is always only the head.

Unfortunately, sometimes in the church local, the eldership thinks that they are the head and this causes trouble because they are not the head, they are the neck. If the neck is not connected to the head then that neck is useless.

In the body of Christ, there is order, there is a government there. Naturally, in ourselves we do not like it. What is our natural life? It is our *self*-life. In our natural life we do not like to be governed; instead, we like to govern others. That was the situation with Adam and Eve in the first place. With that kind of self-life in us it is natural for us to not like government. So when we talk about there being government in the local church we tend to shrink back. But if you really know what government is you will love it. We will also explain this later. God does set up His government in the church local for the sake of building up the body.

Government in the House of God

Let us use another illustration for government in the church. What is the church? The church is the house of God. It is an organic house. In the house there is order. Our Lord Jesus as the Son is over His house. He sets up His government and order in His house. Paul said to Timothy that "I share these things with you that you may know how to behave in the house of God" (I Timothy 3:15). We already are the house of God, but we need to know how to behave or conduct ourselves in the house of God. Do we behave? In the conducting of ourselves in the house of God there is the matter of government there. If you never recognize the government established in the local assembly, you do not know how to behave in the house of God. You need to recognize it.

In Titus 1:5 we read that Paul left Titus to set right things that remained unordered. Here again, we discover there is government, there is order in the house of God. That government and order is according to life.

Government in the Family of God

Another illustration is that the church is the family of God. We are a family. Our Heavenly Father is the father of the family. Our Lord Jesus is the Elder Brother. When the father of a family is there, of course, he is the government. Now if the father is not there then the elder son will take over. Suppose the elder son is not there, then what happens? Well, in the church, in the family of God, you have brothers and sisters, and some are older some are younger. By saying older we mean older spiritually or mature and by saying younger we mean younger spiritually. Naturally, those who are older spiritually will take care of the family. There is order there, there is a government there. Otherwise, it would be chaotic.

Government in the Kingdom of God

We also say the church is a kingdom. If it is a kingdom there must be a king. There must be a government there. So I think it is very clear in the Scripture that there is government in the local assembly. The church is a theocracy, not a democracy. In our natural concept, especially in this country, we think that even the church is a democracy. But no, the church is not a democracy, it is a theocracy. God rules over all as the King, and He has set up His government in His church.

3 — The Development of Local Church Government

Isaiah 9:7a — Of the increase of his government and peace there shall be no end.

Let us go through the book of Acts to discover how government in the local church evolved.

The Twelve Apostles

When our Lord Jesus was on earth He preached to a crowd of many people but then He chose twelve disciples. These twelve were with Him day and night. He trained them for over three years. They were apostles. He trained them in leadership. Even though unfortunately, Judas failed in his leadership in his office, the Holy Spirit confirmed Matthias to be one of the twelve. It is true that Matthias was not chosen by the Lord when the Lord was on earth. However, he was one who followed the Lord from the days of John the Baptist until the Lord was taken up to heaven. He had followed the Lord all these years and was picked by the Holy Spirit as one of the twelve. At the beginning of the book of Acts you have the twelve apostles (Acts 1:16-26). The Lord himself had trained these twelve disciples for over three years. He trained them for government; He trained them for leadership.

The Holy Spirit came down on the day of Pentecost and baptized 120 disciples who were praying with one accord in the upper room. They were baptized in one Spirit into one body*. That is the beginning of the church on earth.

Immediately afterward through the preaching of the gospel of Jesus Christ, the proclamation of His resurrection, 3,000 new believers were added to the church in one day. This is the beginning of the church in Jerusalem—the church local—it started in Jerusalem.

Having now 3,120 members of the body of Christ how do they function? In Acts 2:42 it says, "they persevered, they devoted themselves daily to the teaching and the fellowship of the apostles, to breaking of bread and to prayers." The life within them brought them together. They devoted themselves to *the teaching of the apostles*, which is none other than the teaching of Christ (Matthew 28:20); and *the fellowship of the apostles*, again it is the fellowship of Christ because we are all called into the fellowship of God's Son Jesus Christ (I Corinthians 1:9). They not only have the teaching, but they have the fellowship. They were *breaking bread* together to remember the Lord, to exhibit His victory and to wait for His return (I Corinthians 11:23-26). And they *prayed* together that God's name would be sanctified,

---

* Acts 1:14; 2:1-4; I Corinthians 12:13

3—The Development of Local Church Government

the kingdom would come and God's will would be done on earth as it is in heaven (Matthew 6:9-10; Luke 11:2). They were together as one man. They loved one another. They lived for one another, they lived for Christ. That's the early church, the church in Jerusalem.

But there were so many people. The Lord added to their number daily (Acts 2:47). We figure the church in Jerusalem may have included about 20,000 people. With 20,000 people you have many problems; maybe 20,000 problems or more. With having so many people there needs to be some government for things to not be chaotic. It is true that everybody is holding fast the head, but still for practical reasons the Lord had already provided the government. He had trained the Twelve to be the governing body of the church in Jerusalem.

The Seven

These twelve apostles were not only ministering the word but they also served the tables. They took care of all the brothers and sisters. They were the leaders, they were the governing body, they were prepared beforehand by our Lord for that moment. But it is not the will of God that they should do everything. They discovered this when a problem arose among the widows. They had many widows among them, and the Hellenistic widows were neglected in their supply. Why? Because all these apostles were Hebrew believers. Even though the church in Jerusalem was composed only of Jewish believers, there were two different kinds of Jews as far as cultural background goes. The Hellenistic Jews originally lived in foreign countries where they absorbed the Greek culture and language. The Hebrew Jews lived in the promised land and mainly spoke Hebrew or Aramaic. Since the twelve apostles were all Hebrew Jews they did not know the conditions with the Hellenistic widows. These widows were accidentally neglected and murmuring began to come forth (6:1).

Thank God that problems are good in a sense because they are opportunities if they are solved in the right way. Do not be afraid of problems. As long as we live on earth, there will be problems. As long as there is a local church, there will be problems. But the issue is how to solve them.

These apostles were very sensitive before the Lord. When they heard the rumors they immediately went to the Lord. They then discovered that it was the will of God that they should not monopolize everything in the church. They should instead devote themselves to prayer and to the ministry of God's word (6:4). So they asked the brothers and sisters to come together and said "Choose seven among you full of the Holy Spirit, of good report, and we will establish them over this duty" (6:3). And you know what? All who were chosen were Hellenistic Jews except possibly one. These brothers and sisters had no selfishness in them. If the Hellenistic widows suffered they went overboard and choose all Hellenistic brothers to take care of serving the widows, even if it means that the Hebrew widows may now suffer a little bit accidentally. There was no selfishness among them. And the word of God increased (6:5-7).

These seven were never called deacons. In the Bible, functions come first not titles. If the title comes first, then it becomes a position and it's very dangerous. When you put a person in a position he may think he has authority in himself. So there is no title there at first, it's just a function. These seven did the function of deacons, serving the tables, but they were never called deacons.

The Elders of the Church in Jerusalem

And then persecution came to the church in Jerusalem. You know, these believers in Jerusalem were so happy together, they were so satisfied that they didn't want to leave. They seemed to have forgotten the great commission to go to the nations, disciple all nations, to be His witnesses starting from Jerusalem to Judea to Samaria to the ends of the world (Matthew 28:18-20; Acts 1:8). Thank God, they had such a glorious time together that nobody wanted to leave, and so they forgot the great commission. The church began to look within itself instead of being used as witnesses for the Lord. Then the Lord in His marvelous way allowed persecution to come to the church. And while most of the believers were scattered, strangely, the apostles were not scattered. The apostles stayed behind to continue the work of the Lord there.

With all of these scattered abroad they went to Judea, they went to Samaria and they even went to Gentile cities and the gospel was spread. You would think that Jerusalem was now empty of believers but it was not so. They are still full of believers as you discover in the book of Acts. That's the way it always works. Eventually, Peter and the other apostles began to move out into other cities.

The prophet Agabus foretold by the Spirit that there would be a great famine (Acts 11:28). So, the church in the Gentile world began to send relief to the church in Jerusalem, to the believers in Judea. They sent these contributions by the hand of Paul and Barnabas to the *elders* in Jerusalem (v. 30).

In the beginning, there were the Twelve Apostles, and eventually the Seven were commissioned to function as deacons. Then the apostle Peter began to move out, and the book of Acts does not record all of the footsteps of the apostles. We can believe that other apostles began to move out too because the apostles were originally sent out ones. Afterwards, God began to raise up from the local

3—The Development of Local Church Government

assembly in Jerusalem some other brothers into leadership. When you come to Acts 11:30 you discover there were elders in the church in Jerusalem.

Who were the elders? Of the twelve apostles, we know that only two also served as elders: Peter and John (I Peter 5:1; II John 1:1; III John 1:1). The others never became elders in the local church. Instead, the Lord through the years raised up some brothers who were of spiritual stature, and were able to take responsibility. They became the government of the local church in Jerusalem.

We have not been told how these elders were established but we are told it was a fact. I think that's very, very beautiful. We always like to ask, "How did it come about?" Why? Because we always think of the method, the way, the technical side of things. This is not technical, it is not a method, it is life. It is a manifestation of life, of the Holy Spirit. You do not need to bother about the technical aspects of it. The fact is, there were elders in Jerusalem.

Elders in Local Churches

Those who went out because of the persecution in chapters 8-9 went to Phoenicia, Cyprus and Antioch. And some who were of Cyprian and Cyrenian background began also to preach to the Greeks, the Gentiles. In the beginning, they only preached to the Jews in those cities but eventually, they began to preach to the Gentiles. The Lord saved lots of people, including Gentiles, in Antioch. The news of this came to Jerusalem, and the church in Jerusalem sent Barnabas to go and visit them (11:19-22).

We need to be very careful as we consider this because the church in Jerusalem is not the mother church. It is not the center of all the churches. The church in Antioch is not a daughter church or a sister church. It is an independent church from Jerusalem. But when the church in Jerusalem heard that the Lord had done something in Antioch they wanted to have fellowship with them. They did not desire to go and control them or to pull them into their orbit. Not at all. They wanted to have fellowship with them.

If they sent the apostles there probably there would be some suspicion about control. But they sent a brother there, Barnabas. And this brother had a Hellenistic background, so he understood their background. He was a man with a big heart. He was called the son of consolation (4:36). They sent the right person, not a narrow-minded Judaistic believer who might say things like, "You need to be circumcised. You need to keep the law. And you need to obey the church in Jerusalem." There was no such thing. They sent a brother there to make the fellowship connection, a spiritual affiliation, not an organizational connection. Every local church is independent before God.

3—The Development of Local Church Government

Barnabas went there and saw what the Lord had done. Being himself a teacher he exhorted them to continue on and his ministry strengthened them in the Lord (11:23-24). He soon discovered that it was a larger work than he could do alone. He was such a broad-minded person, a big-hearted man that he went away to Tarsus to find Saul (11:25). Remember that Barnabas was the one who introduced Saul to the leaders in Jerusalem after Saul was converted. Everybody was suspicious of him and dared not touch him. It was Barnabas with the big heart who introduced him (9:26-27). And now again he went to find Saul. He knew Saul was raised up by God and he felt that he could help. There was no selfishness for ministry in the heart of Barnabas. Sometimes someone thinks, "This is my place, I'm here. Don't come. If anybody comes they may want to take over but this is my church!" No, no. That is all wrong of course, it is the church of God, and whatever is good for the church of God Barnabas wanted. His mindset was, "Come, come. Paul, come and help."

These two ministered to the church and to a large crowd a whole year. The church in Antioch was strengthened and the disciples were called Christians first there in Antioch (11:26). Before that time the world thought that these people were only a sect of Judaism. In the eyes of the Roman empire, they were merely a sect of Judaism since at first, they were all Jews or mostly Jews. In Antioch, there were more

Gentiles than Jews so that description didn't fit anymore. What should they call them? One name given in Scripture was *the people of the way* (9:2; 18:26; 19:9, 23; 24:14, 22). Their way of life was different from the world. But in Antioch, they did not know how to define them. Soon people said, "Oh, these people, they are Christians." In the beginning, the word Christian was not an honorable name. It was a nickname. They couldn't figure out who they were, so they said, "Well, who are these people? They are Christ-men." That's what the word Christian means, Christ-ones because with them Christ is everything. Christ is their life, Christ is their everything. So they were called Christians.

The church in Antioch was not started by apostles, they were started by believers who were scattered through persecution. And as a matter of fact, the church in Antioch produced apostles. Today we sometimes wrongfully think that since apostles plant churches, if there is no apostle there is no church. Brothers and sisters, this is not so. It was the church that produced the apostles. When five prophets and teachers were ministering unto the Lord the Holy Spirit said, "Set Me apart Paul and Barnabas for the work that I want them to do." They were sent out as apostles (13:1-4).

Strangely you never find in the book of Acts that there were elders in the church in Antioch. If you find it let me know. Does it mean that there were no elders

3—The Development of Local Church Government

there? No government there? I don't think so. I think it tells us one thing: when brothers and sisters are really holding fast the head, loving one another, walking in the Spirit and functioning as they should, the local church government is hidden. It is there but it is not seen. The government is there but it is as if it is not there. That is the spiritual peak to reach with government in the local church. I think that is probably the reason why the elders are never mentioned there. They still had government there and everything was in order.

We know there must have been elders there in Antioch though not mentioned in Scripture. How do we know? When Barnabas and Paul were sent out by the Holy Spirit to do the work they traveled from place to place and preached the gospel. A number of people were saved. What did these two apostles do after some were saved? Did they stay there with them? No. Actually, they couldn't stay in some places even if they wanted to because they were persecuted and cast out of the city. After these people were saved the apostles left. They left them with the Holy Spirit, left them with the head, left them with God. They went to another place to preach.

And these new believers loved one another, they exhorted one another, they cared for one another while the apostles were away. After some time the apostles came back. In Acts 14, when they came back through the cities, they exhorted them to continue to persevere knowing that we must suffer in order to enter into the kingdom of God (v. 22). They also chose elders in their midst (v. 23). There must have also been elders in Antioch if elders were appointed in all of these new assemblies.

They chose elders as the governing body of the church. Outwardly the apostles chose them, but actually the Holy Spirit appointed them. In Acts 20 Paul told the elders in Ephesus, "The Holy Spirit has appointed you as elders to shepherd the flock of God, the church of God, whom He has bought with His blood" (v.28). During the intervening time of the apostles' visits, these brothers and sisters were together and it became evident that some care, some order, something had to be done, some responsibility had to be taken up. Eventually, some brothers began to show some responsibility. Their seeking of the Lord was more earnest than the others. They seemed to grow a little bit further than the others. The Holy Spirit manifested them as fit to be overseers, and the apostles with their discernment came back and recognized them. It is actually the Holy Spirit who appoints them, not the apostles. This is the way that the government in the local assembly evolved.

Many assemblies begin in homes. The church in Ephesus began in the house of Aquila and Priscilla (I Corinthians 16:19). The church in Colossae began in the house of Philemon (Philemon 1:1-2). The church in Laodicea it begins in the house of Nymphas

3—The Development of Local Church Government

(Colossians 4:15). You find in Rome again it began in the house of Aquila and Priscilla (Romans 16:3-5a). I think it's very natural to begin in a home with a few brothers and sisters. They come together in a house, in a home, like a family. When you are meeting in a home there is not a need for much government. Probably the host of that house will naturally bear most of the responsibility. But as the church begins to increase there will be a need for eldership, there will be a need for government.

That is how government in the local church gradually evolves. It is supernaturally naturally developed.

> Dear heavenly Father, even though we are touching something that is on earth yet we know that it does have its effect in heaven. So we just pray that Thou wilt enable us to approach these things, not with an external, mechanical, or technical concept, but we may really approach it in a living way. Lord, we do pray that Thou wilt show us that Thou art God, the government of the universe, and Thou dost setup Thy government in the church. Show us Thy government that we may know how to behave in Thy house. We ask in the name of our Lord Jesus. Amen.

Part Two: Elders

4 — Delegated Authority

Mark 10:38 — And Jesus said to them, Ye do not know what ye ask. Are ye able to drink the cup which I drink, or be baptised with the baptism that I am baptised with?

When we talk about government in the local church, I hope we will not have a concept of something oppressive that we all try to keep away from. Instead, I feel we need to see government as something that is wonderful, beautiful, full of life and something to be welcomed. We must always remember the government is upon the shoulder of our Lord Jesus. He is the Head of the church. Government belongs to Him and He *is* the government, there is nothing we welcome more after seeing government in this light. So I hope we do not come with a heavy kind of attitude towards government, but see it as God wants us to see it.

When our Lord Jesus was on His way to Jerusalem, in Matthew 20, He shared with His disciples that He would soon be rejected. He shared how He would suffer death in Jerusalem, and after three days be raised from the dead. Strangely, it was after our Lord Jesus had revealed to them that He was going to Jerusalem to die, that the two Sons of

Zebedee, with their mother, came and asked the Lord if they could sit on His right and left in His kingdom. The Lord had just explained to them that He was going to Jerusalem to be crucified, but in the mind of the disciples He was going to Jerusalem to receive His kingdom. This was the mindset not only of these two sons of Zebedee, but also with the rest of the disciples. They all thought He was going to Jerusalem to set up His government upon this earth. They knew He was to be the king of the Jews as well as the king of the whole world. They felt that as far as the kingdom government was concerned this was a critical time. None of these twelve disciples came from a noble background. They had a humble background; and yet during the three years of following the Lord, they were always fighting against each other as to who was the greatest among them. And now at this moment they still had that mindset.

They thought the Lord was going to receive His kingdom, and in the kingdom there would be government. And in the government no doubt the Lord must be the king, but there would be those who sit on His right and on His left. In the old days of China, during the early Chinese empires, they had a similar government. At the head was the emperor, and underneath the emperor were the two prime ministers. We called them the right prime minister and left prime minister. (This would be similar to how

4—Delegated Authority

the secretary of state and secretary of defense are just below the president in the United States.)

The concept of these two positions is that they are just a little bit below the throne, and yet these two are the highest positions in the government. The twelve disciples were trying to get these positions all the time. Now it seemed to be the last possible opportunity and somehow the sons of Zebedee outmaneuvered the other ten. They came and asked for these two positions of authority.

The Lord did not deny there would be someone at the right and left of Him but He said, "Ye do not know what ye ask. Are ye able to drink the cup which I drink, or be baptised with the baptism that I am baptised with?" (Mark 10:38) And these two sons of Zebedee, without any thought or understanding at all, wanted the positions of His right and left so much that they didn't care about the cost. All they wanted was to be in these two positions so they said "Sure, we will." And the Lord said, "Indeed, you will be baptized with My baptism and you will have to drink the cup that I will drink, but to sit on My right and My left is not for Me to give. It is for the Father to give. He will give to those who deserve it" (vv. 39-40). The other ten disciples were very indignant only because they thought they were out maneuvered, not because they thought that it was a wrong request. Actually, they wanted to do the same thing themselves.

While this was all on their minds our Lord Jesus began to teach them about government, rulership and authority. He said, "In this world the great will rule over all, the first will lord over the rest; but this is not true in the kingdom of God. In the kingdom of God, he that wants to be great will be and must be your servant. And he who wants to be the first must be your bondslave. For the Son of man does not come to be ministered to but to minister and to give His life a ransom for many" (vv. 42-45).

Normally, when we talk about government we immediately think of position. We think of authority. We think of ruling. But the Lord said, "What is great? What is first? What is real government? Government is to serve. That's government." We think of ruling as if you are high above everybody and you just rule over everyone else. But the Lord said, "No, true rulership is to be a servant. Not only to be a servant but even to be a bondslave." That is the lowest position you can take. In other words, it is not a matter of position. If you want to seek for a position, alright, you take the *lowest* position, that's government in His kingdom. It is a matter of how much you serve.

Who did the Lord say can serve? All who are baptized with the baptism that the Lord was baptized with, and who drink from the cup that the Lord took. When we think of the cup naturally we think of the Garden of Gethsemane. In the Garden of Gethsemane our Lord Jesus was praying, "Father, if it

4—Delegated Authority

is possible let this cup be removed from Me. But not My will but Thy will be done" (Luke 22:42). While He was praying He sweated so much that the sweat drops came down like blood (v. 44). It was a struggle and the angel had to appear to sustain Him (v. 43). He prayed three times, "Not My will but Thy will be done;" and after He prayed three times He knew it was the cup that the Father had given to Him to drink.

A cup is a portion. The cup represents the will of God. Are you able to drink that cup? Are you willing to accept the will of God whatever it may be? If it is a bitter cup are you willing to drink it? If it is a cup that takes away your dignity are you willing to drink it? Brothers and sisters, are you willing to give up your self, your rights, your everything and accept the will of God for you in all things? Now if you are willing to do that then God will give you authority.

What does it mean to be baptized with the baptism that the Lord was going to be baptised with? In the beginning of His ministry, the Lord went to the River Jordan to be baptized. It was a symbol of entering into death. The reality of that symbol came after three and a half years at Calvary. So the baptism He was referring to was the cross. He was going to the cross to be crucified. Brothers and sisters, are we willing to go to the cross? Are we willing to go into death? death to everything of the world? even ourselves? that we may be raised in resurrection where all is of God and all of Christ? Are we willing to die?

If we do not drink the cup, if we are not being baptized then God is not able to give us authority and government.

When we talk about government we need to change our concept completely. We are not talking about government as it is in this world. In this world government is a position and whoever has the position has the authority; and he, with authority will rule over, lord over other people. But in the church, in the kingdom of God, in the local assembly, government is not a position to be strived after. Government is for those who are willing to go to death, who are willing to accept the will of God in their lives. As this happens, the life of Christ is so manifested in them, that they can serve the church more than anybody else. That is the Lord's concept of government.

It is true that government is for maintaining order. It is to offer leadership. It is to help brothers and sisters to function and be built up together. But in order to do these things it is not a matter of position, it is a matter of spiritual life.

Government in the local assembly is represented by the eldership. Let us remember that Christ is still the Head. He hasn't given up His headship in the church. Though He sets up the elders as the governing body of the local assembly, He has never given up His headship to let the elders take over. This is not so. He is still the Head of the church. He may delegate His authority to the elders but the elders do not substitute

4—Delegated Authority

Him as the Head. I think this is where lots of problems arise. Many problems occur when those who are in leadership feel that they are the head as delegated authorities. They believe they can do anything they think is right, and give orders to the brothers and sisters. Now always remember this thing: Christ is still the Head.

I like to use an illustration for the position of the eldership—they are like the neck, not the head. When Lance Lambert heard this illustration he said "They are the *stiff*-neck." Actually it is often true! There are many necks that are stiff. Why? Because they think that they are the head. Even though our Lord Jesus delegates His authority to some people for the sake of offering leadership, maintaining order and helping the brothers and sisters, they must still remember that He is *the* authority. He may delegate authority to some but He never gives them all authority. He is the only authority in the universe, and He is the authority in the church.

Unfortunately, some people after having been given delegated authority are corrupted by that authority. But why did God give them authority to begin with? It was because they were first submitted to the will of God, they drank the cup, they were baptized with the baptism of the cross. The life of Christ was manifested in them; and on the basis of life authority was given to them. But strangely, that delegated authority has often corrupted people. They forgot about spiritual life and think that they are authority now. Brothers and sisters, we can never be the authority, only God is the authority, only Christ is the authority.

5 — The Plurality of Elders

Titus 1:5 —… and establish elders in each city …

When speaking of local church government, the Bible never mentions elder in the singular number, it is always plural in number—the elders, not the elder. I believe there is a reason for this. If our Lord Jesus as the Head of the church should delegate authority to one person, how easy it would be for that person to think that he is now the head. And how easy it is for the others in the local assembly to misunderstand, thinking that this man is the head of the church and we must obey him in all things. If you have only one man who is at the head of the church, everyone will naturally look to him and think that he is *the* leader he is *the* authority.

Many who really love the Lord, who were used by the Lord originally, have been tempted by this. People look at them as the head, and so they fell into the snare of thinking they are truly the head. A lot of good people are being spoiled since the church looks to them as the head instead of looking upon Christ as the head. Now, of course, the blame is not completely on the brothers and sisters. That person or persons must bear his or their responsibility.

This is why in the Scripture we find such wisdom for having elders always be plural. God never sets up one man as *the* elder in a local church. The elders are always in plural number. Why? Because if you have two or three or more elders, then people's attention will not be focused upon one person. No one person can really represent the Head. It is a corporate leadership. One will be balanced by the others. By maintaining that balance the leadership will be protected from being spoiled. Therefore, elders in the Scripture are always in plural number.

You also do not find presiding elders in the Scripture. We may think, "Yes, the elders are plural, but among the elders there will be the leader of the eldership, the presiding elder, and he is higher than the other elders!" In the Scriptures there is no such setup.

It is true among God's people there is a divine order. Just as in the family you have the parents, you have the older brothers and sisters, you have the younger brothers and sisters; there is an order in the family of God. Whenever God's people are together, if we really live in the life of Christ, if we really walk by the Spirit, inwardly we know there is an order there. I remember brother Watchman Nee used to tell us that when two or three brothers and sisters are together, there is an order there. We need to have the spiritual discernment to know that order. That order is according to spiritual life.

5—The Plurality of Elders

It is true that the life of Christ given to us is given to all equally, but not all receive or develop equally. Due to the different degrees or measure of life in us, when we come together we immediately sense something like, "This brother has a greater measure of Christ in him. He is ahead of me and I need to learn more from him." There is an order, a divine order there. It is not something setup. In a family your older brother is born before you and you naturally know that he is older, and you need to submit yourself to him. So also, among brothers and sisters, even though life is given equally it is not received or developed equally; and because of that, there is a divine order among God's people. The elders are appointed by the Holy Spirit for this very reason, because their life is a little bit more advanced than the others. Therefore, they can exercise oversight with the brothers and sisters.

Suppose there are 5, 7 or more elders among the eldership. They bear responsibility of oversight together, and yet among them there is also an order. It is not an official order that is set up, it is an order of spiritual life and this order changes occasionally. There is no presiding elder, instead the order depends on the measure of Christ among them.

We need to recognize Christ in every brother and sister. This is the reason why the Scripture says "submit to one another in the fear of Christ" (Ephesians 5:21). We need to submit to one another in the fear of Christ. We do not submit to man, we submit to Christ—to the Christ that is in our brothers and sisters. Whenever Christ is manifested through a brother or sister we will submit to the Christ in that individual, no matter how "small" the stature of Christ is, or young in the Lord he or she is. Those who are more advanced in the Lord will manifest Christ more often, and to them we need to submit more. So that is the way of the plurality and order of elders in a local church.

6—The Nature of Eldership

I Timothy 3:1—The word is faithful: if any one aspires to exercise oversight, he desires a good work.

Christ sets up elders in the church to help the growth of the church. When the church is without leadership it is just like a pile of sand spreading out. There is no building up. You need government, you need leadership, you need order for the church to really be built together. This is why our Lord sets up elders as representatives of His government in the church. Remember, it is His government; these elders are just representing His government.

In I Timothy 3 the apostle Paul said, "The word is faithful, if anyone aspires to exercise oversight he desires a good work" (v. 1). If anyone aspires to exercise oversight or if anyone desires to be an elder, he actually desires a good work. What is the nature of eldership? It is not a position you seek after. In III John there was a man called Diotrephes who was ambitious. He desired to be the first among the brothers and sisters, and he somehow took that first position. He became so authoritative that he even denied the apostle John and his coworkers. He ruled the brothers and sisters with an iron hand, and all who did not listen to him were cast out. That was a wrong concept of leadership/ government/ eldership.

If anyone aspires to be an overseer he desires a good work. In other words, eldership is work, a good work. What is good work? The phrase good work in the Scripture simply means doing the will of God. So, eldership is a work, it is not a position. If we aspire to be an elder and we are looking for a position, then we are completely wrong. But if we want to serve our brothers and sisters, if we desire to labor harder than anybody else in the church (I Corinthians 15:10), if we want to be the bondman of all and allow every brother and sister trample upon us, let them throw their burdens upon us—if we desire such a good work, then we can desire to be an elder. Now who wants to be an elder?

Some people want to be elders in the church because they think that to be an elder means they will be above everybody and can be served and give orders. This is not so. In the early centuries, when the early church tried to select people to be a bishop, nobody wanted to be one. Bishops are elders. The term bishop or overseer emphasizes the office and the term elder emphasizes the person. Nobody at that time wanted to be a bishop. They almost had to force some people to be bishops. Why? Because if you are made a bishop it means that you become the servant of all, the bondman of all, everybody will trample upon you. During those times of persecution, usually soon after someone became a bishop, he would be beheaded. Nobody wanted to be a bishop. It is only when the

6—The Nature of Eldership

Holy Spirit constrained a person that he was willing to take that low position of the elder to serve the brothers and sisters. Now that's the Scriptural concept of elders.

Unfortunately, today there is a wrong thought with most of us that the elders are high above all others. The truth is it is an inverted pyramid. The brothers and sisters are high up and the elders are low at the tip. When Paul wrote the letter to the Philippians, he said he wrote the letter to the saints who are in Philippi, the bishops and the deacons. He did not say "to the bishops and the saints," he said "the saints … [and] the bishops and the deacons." The saints come first in order.

On the night of the betrayal of our Lord, He had His last supper with His disciples. He took off His cloak, girded himself with a towel, and washed His disciples' feet. After He finished doing so He said, "You call Me Lord and Master. I am your Lord, I am your Master. I just washed your feet, do likewise." Brothers and sisters, this is government. This is leadership. The Lord said, I do not come to be ministered to, but to minister and to give My life a ransom for all (John 13).

Peter was an elder to the church in Jerusalem as well as an apostle. And he wrote to various elders scattered in other cities: "The elders which are among you I exhort, who am their fellow elder and witness of the sufferings of the Christ, who also am partaker of the glory about to be revealed" (I Peter 5:1-4). Here he calls himself a fellow elder and witness of the sufferings of Christ. Elders and witnesses of the sufferings of Christ are joined together. If you want to be an elder, you are also a witness of the sufferings of the Christ. What does that mean? It means that you are more than someone who can tell others of the sufferings of Christ, but you are one who partakes in the sufferings of Christ. And therefore, your witness is so strong and real.

It is just like the apostle Paul says, "to fill up that which is behind of the afflictions of Christ, for the church which is His body" (see Colossians 1:24). Our Lord Jesus loved the church. He gave himself for her. And after He begot the church He cherishes and nourishes it. He washes it by the water with the word to make the church a glorious church without spot or wrinkle, holy and without blame (see Ephesians 5:23-27). Our Lord Jesus loved the church, and how much He suffered for the church. He suffered for the church in giving up His life on the cross. He suffers for the church now by interceding for us especially (see Hebrews 7:25). When you think of the sufferings of Christ, remember that all these sufferings are because He loves the church. He loves us so much there is almost no end to His suffering; it is an unspeakable, indescribable suffering for us because He loves us.

Those who are in local church government are witnesses of the sufferings of Christ. The love of

6—The Nature of Eldership

Christ so constrains them that they are willing to give their lives for the church. They are willing to fill up that which is behind of the affliction of Christ for the church.

We know that the sufferings of Christ are of two kinds: One is vicarious suffering, that is, He suffered to atone our sins. In that suffering He is all alone by himself. He treads the winepress by himself (Isaiah 63:3). We cannot have any sharing with it. We receive from it but we do not participate in it.

The second area of His suffering is one that He calls us into, that is, the fellowship of His suffering. He wants us to fellowship in His suffering. This is His suffering for the church, His love for the church. He cherishes the church, He nourishes it, He prays for it, that is the eldership.

Do not think that to be an elder is to receive honor and glory today. It is true that Peter said you will receive glory one day, but it is not today. Today all you get is sufferings. If you do not have the mind to suffer (I Peter 4:1) do not aspire to be an elder. When your brothers and sisters misunderstand you, when they blame you for everything in the church can you bear it? Are you able to endure it? Is your love for the church so much that no matter how much you are misunderstood, despised, trampled upon, blamed, ignored, not respected or unnoticed you are still willing to love and serve. You are even willing to serve more just as Paul said, "the less I am loved the more I love" (II Corinthians 12:15). That is the nature of government. That is the nature of eldership.

7—How to Exercise Oversight

I Peter 5:1-4—The elders which are among you I exhort, who am their fellow-elder and witness of the sufferings of the Christ, who also am partaker of the glory about to be revealed: shepherd the flock of God which is among you, exercising oversight, not by necessity, but willingly; not for base gain, but readily; not as lording it over your possessions, but being models for the flock. And when the chief shepherd is manifested ye shall receive the unfading crown of glory.

How do you exercise oversight? The apostle Peter said, "Shepherd the flock of God which is among you." The elders are shepherds. They shepherd the flock of God. Our Lord Jesus is the good shepherd (John 10). The good shepherd gives His life for His sheep. Our Lord Jesus is the Great Shepherd of the flock; and by the blood of His eternal covenant He matures us (Hebrews 13:20). Our Lord is the Chief Shepherd of the flock (I Peter 5:4). Elders in the church are *under*-shepherds. They are shepherds of the flock of God.

And if you want to know how to shepherd the flock, read Psalm 23 "The Lord is my shepherd, I shall not want …" That is the work of the shepherd. The shepherd will lead the sheep; find the green pasture; protect the sheep; set the table before the sheep; anoint the head of sheep—He will do everything for the sheep. That is shepherding.

How do you do it? By "exercising oversight, not by necessity but willingly." When you exercise oversight, it is because of love not because of duty. If it is a position, then it carries some kind of notation of duty. If you take the eldership as a position, then it is your duty to do it. Whether you like it or not you have to do it. But eldership is not duty, it is more than duty—it is love. So, it is not by necessity but they do so willingly.

"Not for base gain but readily." You are not trying to have that position in order that you may gain fame or name or power or whatever for yourself. No, it is not for gain. But it is readily. You are always ready to give, not to gain, but to give.

"Not lording over your possessions but being models for the flock." Do not consider God's people as your possessions. We often hear people say "my flock" as if God's people are someone's possessions. They are not your possession they belong to God. Therefore, you cannot lord over them as if they are your possessions, as if you can do anything that you would like to. They are not yours, you are just a steward, a servant, a bondslave called by God to serve the flock of God. What then should you do? You should be an example, a model for the flock.

7—How to Exercise Oversight

The shepherd usually goes before the sheep. He is their role model. And all the elders should be models for the flock. As a matter of fact, if you look at the elders you would be able to know what kind of a flock they have, because they are the models of the flock.

And it is only "when the Chief Shepherd of the sheep" returns then those who are faithful in serving Him will "receive the unfailing crown of glory."

8 — The Qualifications of Elders

I Timothy 3:1-7 — The word is faithful: if any one aspires to exercise oversight, he desires a good work. The overseer then must be irreproachable, husband of one wife, sober, discreet, decorous, hospitable, apt to teach; not given to excesses from wine, not a striker, but mild, not addicted to contention, not fond of money, conducting his own house well, having his children in subjection with all gravity; (but if one does not know how to conduct his own house, how shall he take care of the assembly of God?) not a novice, that he may not, being inflated, fall into the fault of the devil. But it is necessary that he should have also a good testimony from those without, that he may fall not into reproach and the snare of the devil.

Titus 1:5-9 — For this cause I left thee in Crete, that thou mightest go on to set right what remained unordered, and establish elders in each city, as I had ordered thee: if any one be free from all charge against him, husband of one wife, having believing children not accused of excess or unruly. For the overseer must be free from all charge against him as God's steward; not headstrong, not passionate, not disorderly through wine, not a striker, not seeking gain by base means; but hospitable, a lover of goodness, discreet, just, pious, temperate, clinging to the faithful word according to the doctrine taught, that he may be able both to encourage with sound teaching and refute gainsayers.

What are the qualifications of the elders? If you go to I Timothy 3 and Titus 1, you discover a lot of qualifications are mentioned there. We will not go over these qualifications one by one, but we will look at them together as a group.

First, let me say that the lists both in Timothy and in Titus are a little bit different; so keep in mind these are not exhaustive lists, they are only illustrative lists. They give us some illustration of what kinds of qualities God is looking for in an elder. It is not a complete list. You do not go over this list one by one and say "Now, I'm qualified for this, I am not qualified for that." It is not for that purpose. Even if you are qualified for every one of them you may not be qualified. It is not an exhaustive list, but it is there to give an impression of what kind of persons God is looking for who will take care of His own flock. Our Lord loves His flock so much that He wants to commit His flock to good and right men. And these are the qualities He is looking for.

8—The Qualifications of Elders

Strangely, in the world when they want to have some work accomplished, when they employ a person to do a certain job, what do they look for? They look at his education, his experience, his abilities, his skills and see if he is qualified to do the job. His character, his lifestyle and relationships are very minor, and sometimes they don't even bother about them. That's the situation in the world; but in the house of God, when God is trying to find some people who will represent Him in His church, represent His authority, exercise oversight for Him, represent His government, what's He looking for? If you read these two lists you see the qualifications are predominantly matters of character, not of ability. Only two in the whole list may be considered as abilities: (1) governs his household well. If you govern your own house well then you can govern the house of God. That is ability more than character. (2) Apt to teach. You have that kind of aptitude to teach. Whether in public or in personal counseling. Now these two are the only abilities listed there. All the rest are concerned with character, with what kind of a man you are.

Do not think that these items listed are just morality. You can find in the world some people who are so moral that they can fit into most of these lists. No, these are not just man-made morality, these are manifestations of Christ being formed in their lives. It is not our natural temperament or morality, it is the remaking of our character. We are characterized with the character of Christ. That is what the Lord is looking for in an elder, in one who will take oversight over the flock of God.

So, you see again it is a matter of life. It is a matter of life more than gift, more than talent, because spiritual life is the thing that He is looking for. He is conforming us to the image of Christ. Image is related to character. When is the church built? When the character of Christ is manifested, then the church is built. It is not built by being so well organized, so successful, with so many people or activities. No, the church is built when Christ is formed. Therefore, character is the thing that you look for in an elder.

To be an elder you also need to have vision. By vision we mean you need to know the eternal purpose of God. Without vision the people disintegrate (Proverbs 29:18). How can you lead the people? How can you unite the people? How can you direct the people? How can you help and console the people? How are you going to build them together unless you have vision? You must know what the Lord is doing, you need to know what the Lord is after; otherwise, how can you lead? How can you direct? How can you help? An elder needs to be a person who has vision.

Sometimes we say so-and-so has a vision, a dream. Or we may say, Well, so-and-so has a vision that God wants him to be a missionary in a foreign land, to evangelize the world, or open an orphanage or school or whatever it may be. No, we are not talking about that. We are talking about in the heart and mind of God. He has purposed a purpose in His Son and for His Son (Ephesians 1:9, 3:11). He has been working throughout the ages for that purpose on His heart to be realized. That is the vision you must have. Otherwise, you do not know where to lead God's people to. That purpose, put very simply, is Christ and the church. That is the heavenly vision that Paul saw on the road to Damascus. That is the vision that John saw on the island of Patmos: the seven lampstands and Christ in the midst of them—Christ and the church. We need to see in our spirit. This is the mystery of God. This is the mystery of Christ that has been revealed; and we need to receive the spirit of wisdom and revelation for that vision. This is for the building of the church.

9—How Elders are Chosen

Acts 14:23—And having chosen them elders in each assembly, having prayed with fastings, they committed them to the Lord, on whom they had believed.

How does the eldership come about? Strangely, even though the Scripture says the apostles chose elders it was not that way in every case. We really do not know how the elders come into being in all of the different places. It seems as if God is not bound by any rigid method or way. But one thing is certain, the elders are appointed by the Holy Spirit. The Holy Spirit appoints elders on what basis? Based on the measure of Christ in that person. The Holy Spirit is always glorifying Christ.

Then why did the apostles confirm it? I personally feel it is for the weak among God's people. If you really live with the life of Christ, if you really walk in the Spirit, you should be able to sense within yourself those whom God has chosen to take the oversight. You simply know it. The Holy Spirit will manifest these people to you. Only those who are spiritually weak need something external to help them to know who the overseers are. Actually, you do not find in every case that the apostles laid hands on the elders and ordained them, as it were, to be elders. No, even when apostles chose them and prayed over them, they did not ordain them. The elders are divinely ordained by the Holy Spirit.

So the whole matter again is a spiritual matter. It is a matter of life. If God's people really live in the life of Christ and under the rule of the Holy Spirit, then when we come together and gather for a while, naturally those who are more advanced in spiritual life and upon whom God has put more responsibility, out of love, will begin to serve more diligently and take care of the brothers and sisters. Whenever you have problems you know who to go to, nobody needs to tell you this is the responsible brother you need to go to. You know who to go to naturally because you know that that person can help you in the Lord. In this way the elderhood is manifested. Are you able to accept this? Do you need to see an outward position given to someone before you can recognize their spiritual role of responsibility? That tells a lot about your life. If you really live in the Spirit, you don't need these external, official things. You know who to submit to.

So, I will not tell you how you choose the elders, whether you choose the elder by vote or secret ballot or whatever it is. I will leave it with the Holy Spirit and I hope you all will leave it to the Holy Spirit.

10 — The Saints and Elders

Acts 15:22-23 — ... it seemed good to the apostles and to the elders, with the whole assembly ... The apostles, and the elders, and the brethren ...

Philippians 1:1 — Paul and Timotheus, bondmen of Jesus Christ, to all the saints in Christ Jesus who are in Philippi, with the overseers and ministers [deacons] ...

What is the relationship between the elders and the brothers and sisters? In the world, the government and those who are governed somehow are separated. True, in the United States, it is the "government of the people, by the people and for the people;" but somehow you find once the government is set up it is also *above* the people. There is a separation there. That's why I say authority will spoil a person. Having a position spoils the person. When you are given a position it spoils you, it makes you think that you are greater, higher and above others. But again, in the church it is not a matter of position. If you want to talk about position it is the lowest position.

There is a close relationship between the local church government and the brothers and sisters in the local assembly. They are never separated. Those who are responsible for the church must seek the Lord for His mind and will on everything. They are not the Head, they look up to the Head to discover from the Head His mind for His people. And oftentimes the way they find the mind of the Head is through the body—through the brothers and sisters. Those leaders in the local church should always be in contact, in communication with the brothers and sisters. They are to hear from the body the mind of Christ. They find from the body the needs and bring these needs to the Head. Again, it's just like the neck. Everything from all the different members goes through the neck and to the Head; and then finds the mind of the Head and from the Head comes back to the whole body. Outwardly, it seems that these elders decide for the church the things to be done or not to be done, what should be done and what should not be. Outwardly, it looks like that; but actually, it is decided by the body under the Head.

I think Acts 15 is a clear example of this principle. When there was a problem the apostles and elders did not just come together and say, "Alright, there is a problem so let's talk about it and make a decision about it." No, when there was a problem in the church they opened it up to the whole church. Every brother and sister had a chance to express how he or she felt about the matter (though, not in the flesh of course). And then these elders and apostles took the feelings of the body to the Lord and sought the Head about it.

10—The Saints and Elders

By the time the decision was made, they said, "The Holy Spirit and we decide …" So there must be a real coordination, connection, communication between the responsible brothers, or those in responsibility, and the brothers and sisters. They should never be separated.

One problem today is that some elders think they can decide for the rest of the people on everything. They believe they can just give the order and everybody has to do it. This is not true. They must learn to get the feeling from the body in order to bring it to the Head; and then get from the Head His mind for the body. So, there is a close relationship between the local church government and the brothers and sisters in the local assembly. There is no division at all.

11—Elders in the Time of Recovery

> Revelation 3:7a—And to the [messenger] of the assembly in Philadelphia write

What form, if any, of local church government should we take in the time of recovery? Today we are in the time of the recovery of the house of God. Before our Lord returns, the church must be recovered to the original purpose of God. Through the centuries the church has fallen. It has become an earthly institution. But we believe that God is doing the work of recovery. He is recovering His church back to where He originally desired for it to be. Now in the time of recovery, what about this matter of eldership, of government? On the one hand, we believe that in the recovery work God is doing He desires to recover government in the local church. Spiritual authority must be recovered. God's people must know authority and submission. Divine order in the house must be recovered. We believe this.

Yet, on the other hand, we feel there is a real problem with recovering the outward form of local church government. If you want to recover eldership are you able to? In the first place, God's people are so divided. They are no longer one. We say the church is one, one universally and one locally, but actually,

God's people are divided into pieces and bits and fragments. How are you going to put them together?

You know that we are one body and thus we should not be divided. Everybody knows that. There is the ecumenical movement that is trying to help the church come together by compromising, agreeing to disagree, and disagreeing to agree. They try to maintain an outward unity. Is this the unity that God is recovering? When our Lord Jesus prayed that prayer in John 17 He said, "that they may be one as You [the Father] and I are one." It is not an outward union. It is an inward unity that God is looking for.

If you go to a virgin land, and there are no Christians there, you may preach the gospel, gather a people together unto the Lord, and then you are able to recover the local church there not only in reality but also in name. You can call it the church in that certain place. But today you cannot do that. You cannot call yourselves the church in Richmond today. Why? Because there are many of God's people in Richmond who are not gathering together with you. There are many brothers and sisters in many different denominations. There are many brothers and sisters in many different groups, many fellowships and many home meetings. Brothers and sisters, we are one in Christ, we should be one in practice. But can we gather all together like in the early church in Jerusalem? We are not able to do that. That is why we cannot call ourselves the church in Richmond.

11—Elders in the Time of Recovery

Because the church in Richmond includes all God's people in Richmond. Thank God for that.

Then what are we doing here? Well, that is the principle of recovery. We are standing on the ground of the unity of the body of Christ. We refuse to be divided, we come together under the Headship of Christ. We have no other name but the name of Christ. We learn to put ourselves under His authority. We treasure His presence. We allow Him to be our Head, and we open our hearts and hands to all God's people in Richmond. This is our testimony. That's all we can do. And that's what God wants us to do.

Despite all the difficulties, the testimony of the unity of the body of Christ has to be maintained. Now because of this we have a problem. Can we appoint elders today? Can we give people titles as elders? You know, in recovery it seems to me that God is no longer looking for outward things, He is looking for the inward reality. In other words, it is no longer the title or the office of elder that He is looking for; it is the function of the elders He is after. In the beginning of the church this is what the eldership was. It was a function and that can still be recovered.

You can compare the two sets of 7 letters written to the churches: one set written by Paul the other written (or transcribed) by John. In the 7 letters written by Paul, though there are problems, God still recognized that the church is in its normal state. In those 7 churches you have deacons and elders or bishops. But when you come to the 7 letters of John in Revelation chapters 2 and 3, these are written to the messenger of the church. In Philippians Paul is able to write to the saints in Philippi, the bishops and the deacons; but in Revelation chapters 2 and 3 it is written to the messenger of the church in Ephesus, in Smyrna, in Pergamos, in Thyatira, in Sardis, in Philadelphia and in Laodicea. Who are the messengers? We know the word messenger can refer to two different kinds of messengers. They can be celestial messengers, which are angels; or they can be terrestrial messengers, men. In this case, we feel they are not celestial messengers since the Lord would not write to the angels as He writes to the church on earth. They must refer to men as messengers. These have no title; they are not called elders, just messengers. Those who receive messages from the risen Head and deliver them to the people. They are like stars in the right hand of the risen Lord (Revelation 1:20). They have a heavenly life, they have the life of Christ in them as light shining in darkness. And they are in the hand of the Lord himself. The Lord is supporting them as they are responsible to the Lord for the local assembly. They have no position, no title—theirs is a spiritual function. They function as those who are responsible for the church in Ephesus.

Brothers and sisters, does it mean that today in the recovery work of God the function of government, the function of elders must be recovered? Yes. As a

11—Elders in the Time of Recovery

matter of fact, it must be. Wherever God's people are together there must be some people who function as elders, but there is no title for them, there is no outward position. Since there is no title and no position it is more difficult to function; but that proves whether you are chosen by the Lord or not.

Again, as you read I Timothy and II Timothy you see such a difference between these two letters which were written only a few years apart. Paul wrote his first letter to Timothy after he was released from the Roman prison in AD 63-64. He then came to Ephesus again and saw that the church was there but without any elders. Many years earlier, he had established elders in Ephesus and for three years lived and ministered there. Then while in prison for two years he wrote the letter to the Ephesians. Now that he came back to Ephesus, after being released from prison, those original elders that were appointed before weren't there anymore. So new elders had to be chosen. Having no time to remain with them he left Timothy there and shared with him by letter "how one ought to conduct oneself in the house of God" (I Timothy 3:15). In 1st Timothy he called the church "the house of the living God, the pillar and the base of truth." Also, in that letter he tells us the qualifications of the elders and of the deacons.

Only a few years later when writing his second letter to Timothy the whole situation there had changed. In AD 64 Nero burned the city of Rome and put the blame on the Christians. They were the scapegoats. The whole atmosphere changed. If you were a Christian you were a criminal in the sight of the government. Christians were persecuted and killed; everything had changed. Paul wrote the 2nd letter to Timothy before his martyrdom. He had been arrested again, brought to Rome and put in the dungeon, waiting to be sentenced and beheaded. He knew it was coming. When he wrote this 2nd letter he said "all Asia has forsaken me" (1:15). He labored years in Asia Minor and they forsook him. It was too difficult for them. They may have not left the Lord, but they left him. During his first trial no one would defend him, everybody hid themselves lest they also be arrested (4:16). It was a difficult time for the believers; don't blame them. So, he stood alone, but the Lord was with him. Everything had changed so when Paul mentioned the church he said, "The Lord knows who are His. Let those who will call upon the name of the Lord depart from iniquity. But in a great house there are vessels of gold and silver, and vessels of wood and clay. There are vessels of honor and vessels to dishonor. Purify yourself from these vessels of dishonor that you may be a vessel of honor fit for the Master's use. Gather with those who are faithful" (2:19-22).

The church is no longer called "the house of the living God;" it has now become "a great house." It is no longer pure, there are now vessels of honor as well

11—Elders in the Time of Recovery

as vessels of dishonor. Gold and silver describes some believers: gold being the nature of God and silver representing the redemption of Christ. There were people who lived by the life of Christ in them. But there are also now ones who are the Lord's and yet live by their own flesh. Wood represents man and earthen clay stands for the work of man. The calling now is to purify ourselves. Don't be a vessel to dishonor the Lord. Don't live in your flesh. Don't work in the energy of your natural man. Depart from iniquity, live by the life of Christ within, and be faithful to the very end. What a change! In the church, it is no longer a matter of outward appearance it is now especially a matter of inward reality.

So, I have wondered how today in the recovery work of God, government in the local church is to be recovered. Unfortunately, in many groups there is a type of democracy, but it is really anarchy. There is no order, no discipline. There is no government, no coordination. How can the church be built? May God raise up some for the love of the church willing to give themselves to the church. May He raise some up who will give up their lives to represent Christ the Head, and to serve the brothers and sisters. These are those who without any name, without any title, without any position, are misunderstood, trampled upon, but faithfully serving the Lord, serving the brothers and sisters, taking care of the house of God. Brothers and sisters, this is a must.

May the Lord raise up people who will function as elders, take the lowest place and serve, lead and suffer. But do not look for a title. Do not look for a position. I believe this will deliver us from being corrupted by the power of recognized position. I wonder if this is the way of the Lord for His church today. I just want to share it with you. Take it to the Lord and see whether this is the way of the Lord concerning local government. Shall we pray.

Dear heavenly Father, we humble ourselves before Thee, acknowledging to Thee that either we have not been for government or we have corrupted Thy government. We pray Lord that Thou wilt reveal to us Thy concept of government. We pray that Thou wilt raise up some who are willing to take the oversight for the sake of Thy people. We pray that in this recovery of government in the local church it may be of life and not an organization.

Lord, we pray that Thou wilt open the eyes of the people to recognize the government that Thou wilt setup in Thy church; that we may know how to behave in the house of God. Teach us how to submit to one another in the fear of Christ; that the divine order in the church may be setup to the glory of God and the building up of the church. Lord, our prayer is that Thy church be built, made ready for Thee our King, our Bridegroom, our Head. We ask in the name of our Lord Jesus. Amen.

Part Three: The Ministry of the Word

12—Body Ministry

Ephesians 4:15-16—holding the truth in love, we may grow up to him in all things, who is the head, the Christ: from whom the whole body, fitted together, and connected by every joint of supply, according to the working in its measure of each one part, works for itself the increase of the body to its self-building up in love.

To begin with, let us be very clear that the will of God is for every member of the body of Christ to be involved in ministry. Ministry is not something that is only to be done by a few. The will of God is that every member of the body of Christ must function and minister one to another for the growth of the body. The reason local churches today are so weak and do not grow as they should is because they rely upon one or a few to minister. Instead, let us see that every member of the body of Christ must be involved in ministry.

It is true that God has laid upon some people the work of the ministry of the word. In Ephesians 4:11 we read, "and he has given some apostles, and some prophets, and some evangelists, and some shepherds and teachers." This is the ministry of the Word. But these people are "for the perfecting of the saints" (v.12). That is, these people are God's gift to his church to perfect the saints, to mature the saints—to help the saints to grow, or in some versions it reads equip the saints—that these may be equipped. And after they are perfected, matured and equipped they begin to function and fulfill the ministry of the body. This is called body ministry. Body ministry comes out of the body; and it is for the body. Every brother and sister should be involved in body ministry. Every member of the body must function according to the grace and gift that God has given to each one of them.

Unless we see every member of the body functioning, we do not really see the church. So I hope that when we are talking about local ministry we do not think that we are not involved. As a matter of fact, everyone should be involved.

Ephesians 4:15-16 shows that as all the members of the body grow up into the Head—that is, Christ—every member will function and work according to the measure of each part, for the self-building up of the body in love. As we are joined to the Head, as we hold fast the Head, as we grow into Christ the Head, then the whole body—every member—begins to minister one to another. And the result is the body is built in love.

In Colossians 2:19 we read of this same body ministry experience: "... holding fast the head, from whom all the body, ministered to and united together by the joints and bands, increases with the increase of God."

Then too, I Corinthians 12, we read that even though there is one body, yet there are many members. Even though there are many members, yet there is one body. Even though all the members of the body are different—they are given different gifts according to the measure of the Holy Spirit (because gifts are the manifestations of the Holy Spirit)—yet all these members are needed. Every member must be living and functioning, so the body will not be paralyzed. And as all these members begin to function and contribute to the welfare of the body, the body is built, and being matured.

So, first of all, I would like to lay this foundation, this fundamental principal: that every member of the body of Christ is to function. If we are the Lord's, if we are saved, if we have the life of Christ, if the Holy Spirit dwells in us and He has given us particular gifts, then we ought to minister one to another. With this body ministry, the church will increase with the increase of God.

13—The Ministry of God's Word

Acts 6:4—but we will give ourselves up to prayer and the ministry of the word.

In I Corinthians 14:26, when all the brothers and sisters are assembled together, that is when the church meets, it says *each one has*: One has a tongue, one has a teaching, one has an interpretation, one has a revelation. Let everything be done for the edification of the body of Christ. So each brother and sister ought to bring something to the church for its increase. Every one of us can edify, exhort, encourage, console and comfort. This is something that everyone can be and must be involved in. This is body ministry.

Now knowing this, then we move on to this matter of local ministry. The local ministry that we are talking about is a little bit different than body ministry. We are not talking about the body ministry which everybody is involved in. We are not talking about the exhortation, encouragement, and consolation that everybody may have a part in (I Corinthians 14:3); but we are talking about the ministry of the word of God in any given local assembly.

Before we look specifically into the ministry of the word of God in each local assembly, let us first talk about the ministry of the word on a larger horizon.

> ... but we will give ourselves up to prayer and the ministry of the word (Acts 6:4).

The twelve apostles were ministering the word of God to the people of God in the early church in Jerusalem. But at the same time, they had to serve the tables for the widows, that is, to take care of the widows and their needs. We then find that both ministries suffer. Because of a problem of accidental negligence, they realized that it was not God's will for them to monopolize everything in the house of God. God had intended for different ones to do different works. They asked the brothers and sisters to choose seven men to take care of serving the widows. And the apostles then said "we will devote ourselves to prayer and the ministry of the word."

> Therefore, having this ministry, as we have had mercy shewn us, we faint not (II Corinthians 4:1).

Paul mentions something here of the ministry of God's word. Now the ministry that he is talking about is not the body ministry. The ministry he is talking about is the ministry of the word of God. That is the ministry he is especially called to fulfill.

13—The Ministry of God's Word

> … and he has given some apostles, and some prophets, and some evangelists, and some shepherds and teachers, for the perfecting of the saints; with a view to the work of the ministry (Ephesians 4:11-12b).

Here we discover that God does raise up some people for the ministry of His word. This "work of the ministry" is the ministry of God's word. Our Lord Jesus, after He died and was resurrected, He gave gifts to men (v.8, 11). He gave to the church some apostles, some prophets, some evangelists, some pastors and teachers. These four classes of people are the gifts from the Head of the church to His body for the sake of perfecting the saints. And as a matter of fact, you will find these four classes of men are ministers of the word of God. They are involved with the ministry of the word of God.

> And now I commit you to God, and to the word of his grace, which is able to build you up and give to you an inheritance among all the sanctified (Acts 20:32).

Why is it that the ministry of the word of God is so important? In Acts chapter 20 the apostle Paul feeling within himself an urgency to arrive at Jerusalem before Pentecost, bypassed Ephesus. This was a church that he loved so much, and had spent so much of his time and himself with. But he was afraid that if he should visit Ephesus on his way to Jerusalem, he would be delayed. He would not be able to get away from the saints that easily. So instead of going to Ephesus, he called the elders in Ephesus to come to Miletus, and there he shared his heart with them. He said, "You may never see me again, but I commit you to God and to the word of His grace that will build you up." So, brothers and sisters, how is the church built? The church is built by the word of Grace, which is the word of God. And that is the reason why the ministry of the word is so essential to the church for its building up.

14 — The Ministers of the Word

Ephesians 4:8-12 — Wherefore he says, Having ascended up on high, he has led captivity captive, and has given gifts to men. But that he ascended, what is it but that he also descended into the lower parts of the earth? He that descended is the same who has also ascended up above all the heavens, that he might fill all things; and he has given some apostles, and some prophets, and some evangelists, and some shepherds and teachers, for the perfecting of the saints; with a view to the work of the ministry, with a view to the edifying of the body of Christ.

Our risen and ascended Lord loved the church and gave gifts to the church: He gave four classes of men.

The Apostles

Apostleship technically is not a gift but an office. In other words, God has called some people and sent them out for a specific mission; and the mission is to plant the church. These are the functions of apostles. Their functioning is specifically for the church universal rather than the church local. In the letter to the Ephesians Paul has the church universal in mind: "… the church, which is his body, the fulness of him that filleth all in all" (1:22b-23 ASV). Ephesians has the church universal in mind; so when speaking of these four classes of men, the apostles are for the church universal specifically. As they are sent out, naturally they travel. They go from place to place to plant the churches of God. Peter traveled around as all the apostles travel around.

The Evangelists

And then we have the evangelists. We do not know what the gift of the evangelist is, but we know the work of the evangelist. He is to travel to different localities spreading the gospel of Jesus Christ, and bringing people into the kingdom of God. These are evangelists. So the evangelist is also for the church universal and they travel extensively.

For example, Philip in Acts 8. Remember the Seven who served the tables for the widows? (Acts 6) One of them was Phillip. But because of the persecution in Jerusalem many of the believers dispersed and scattered; so there was no need for people to remain there to serve the tables. Phillip traveled to Samaria. He was an evangelist (Acts 21:8). And God used him mightily in Samaria. But at the very time when the work in Samaria seemed to be so successful, suddenly, the Holy Spirit took Philip out

14—The Ministers of the Word

of Samaria and said "You go south on the way to Gaza which is in the desert."

Now think of it. An evangelist should be where lots of people are. The more people, the more opportunity to spread the gospel. And yet the Holy Spirit has His own plan. He took Philip out of Samaria and sent him to the desert. Philip knew the Holy Spirit. He obeyed. I'm afraid probably today, some will plan their trips by the crowds—where they can gain an audience, that's where they go to. But as a matter of fact, the Holy Spirit is the planner of God's work. So Philip obeyed God, left Samaria and went down on the road to Gaza in the desert. And, lo and behold, there was a eunuch from Ethiopia returning from worshiping in Jerusalem. He was on his chariot reading the Bible. The Holy Spirit said to Philip, "Run alongside that chariot." And he ran alongside. Think of that.

Then Philip asked that man, "What are you reading?"

And he said, "I am reading Isaiah." It was Isaiah chapter 53.

"Do you understand?" Philip asked him.

He said, "I don't. I do not know who the writer refers to—whether he refers to a nation or whether he refers to a person. Who is the one who bears our sorrows, our iniquities, our sins? The one who was crushed?"

So he asked Philip to come on the chariot. And Philip explained to him the Lord Jesus was the One in Isaiah 53. As he shared the gospel with him the eunuch accepted the Lord.

When they came to the place where there was water in the desert, (which was a very rare thing), the Eunuch asked, "Is there any obstacle for me to be baptized? I want to belong to Christ." And Philip baptized him.

The Spirit of God took Philip away; and the eunuch went on his way rejoicing. The eunuch had lost Philip, but he had gained Christ.

Then Philip appeared in Azotus, which is one of the cities of the Philistines. He traveled through the cities until finally you find him in Caesarea. So the evangelist is one who moves around, just like the apostles travel around.

The Prophets

And then you have the prophets and the teachers. Brothers and sisters, it seems to me the prophets and the teachers are both for local ministry and for universal ministry. If you read the book of Acts, you will find that the apostles and the evangelists seem to be traveling around, but the prophets and the teachers stay in one place sometimes and at other times they travel.

14—The Ministers of the Word

The emphasis with prophets in the New Testament is not in foretelling—predicting events—but in forthtelling. Prophets are those who receive revelation and know the mind of God. They share with God's people what God's mind is, what God thinks of them, what God is going to do with them and what the ultimate purpose of God with them is. That is a prophet's ministry.

Today people think that a prophet is one who prophesies—that is foretelling—telling you that you should marry some specific person. Or that you should do this or that. I do not say that in the New Testament a prophet is never used of God to tell an individual what the will of God is for him. Yet I do say, that even so, in the New Testament times, it is rare. And if it is done, it is only for confirmation or for correction, never for direction.

Why the difference? In the Old Testament time, the Holy Spirit hadn't come yet. So how could people know the mind of God? How did they know the will of God? There were only a few ways. One was to go to the high priest. The high priest had on his chest the breastplate. And on that breastplate there were these twelve precious stones with the names of the twelve tribes inscribed on it. Then there was a pocket with two things: urim and thummim—light and perfection. When the high priest entered into the holiest of all to appear before God, he sought to find the mind of God for the nation. Somehow on the breastplate something happened that would reveal the mind of God for his people. Now, we really do not know exactly how the urim and thummim worked. Some people say these two stones actually complete the alphabet of the Hebrew alphabet. And when the high priest came before the presence of God, the light began to move upon these stones and spell out the mind of God. That's what some people say. We do not know for sure. And other people say these two stones actually are lots; and you cast the lot and you'll know either yes or no. Again, we really don't know. But in the Old Testament time, this was one way to know the mind of God.

But they didn't go to the high priest for very small personal matters. The high priest only went to the Lord in matters that were concerning the whole nation. Unfortunately, the stones were lost. So during the reign of Cyrus the king of Persia, when the children of Israel returned to Jerusalem to rebuild the temple, there was no high priest with the urim and thummim. They could not decide on many things. They had to wait until those stones were returned to the high priest in Jerusalem.

That is one way in the Old Testament to know the mind of God. And there is another way: God raised up seers or prophets. These seers or prophets were like Samuel. In I Samuel chapter 9 we read that Saul was looking for the lost donkeys of his father. He couldn't find them but knew that Samuel the seer was

14—The Ministers of the Word

nearby. He went to ask Samuel what happened to the donkeys. When Saul met Samuel, Samuel told him the donkeys were already home and his father was worried concerning him. Samuel was a seer, a prophet. During the Old Testament times they went to the prophets and were told what to do.

And there is another way of knowing the mind of God in the Old Testament, which is the law of God, the Torah. They could read God's word and—through the Torah—understand His will.

Therefore, we see in the Old Testament times, while the Holy Spirit hadn't come yet, that the ordinary people had no way to know the mind of God by themselves. They had to consult a seer, a prophet, or a high priest. But in the New Testament times, under the New Covenant, you do not need anyone to tell you the mind of Christ. What is the New Covenant? In the New Covenant, you do not need anyone to tell you 'know the Lord.' Why? Because, from the smallest of you to the greatest of you, you shall know Him in yourselves (Hebrews 8). Why? Because the Holy Spirit has come. The Spirit of God has come. The Spirit of Christ has come. He now dwells in each one of the believers. If you are a child of God, you have the Holy Spirit dwelling in your new spirit. And the Holy Spirit will teach you all things. You do not need some outside teaching because He teaches you from within, if you listen.

Sometimes when He speaks there's a still small voice; sometimes His speaking is like the putting on of an ointment—a moving within you; sometimes it is like a light begins to burst within you; sometimes it is just a deep sense of peace. It is the Holy Spirit who is teaching you, who is telling you what you should do. It is God who directly leads you.

So in the New Testament times God does raise up prophets but these prophets are not to direct your life. Your life is so precious to Christ. He will not leave your souls to any person. He will take care of you himself. The prophets today are to tell you the mind of God, the purpose of God, the will of God for His people. Very rarely will they tell somebody, "This is what you should do." And if they do it, remember, it is not to direct your life. It is either to confirm what the Holy Spirit has already told you or to correct, because you may misunderstand the Holy Spirit. They should never direct your life.

God does raise up the prophets to tell us the mind of God by revelation—not revelation extra to the Bible—but by revelation of the Word of God.

The Shepherds and Teachers

The teachers are more occupied with the understanding of the word of God. As they study the word of God, He gives them understanding of the word, so they can expound it and explain it to us.

14—The Ministers of the Word

Teachers are combined with pastors or shepherds: "some pastors and teachers." Pastors and teachers are one person, not two. They all deal with the word of God. One aspect is teaching publicly; and the other is counseling privately—shepherding.

15 — Local Ministry of the Word

Acts 13:1-4—Now there were in Antioch, in the assembly which was [there], prophets and teachers: Barnabas, and Simeon who was called Niger, and Lucius the Cyrenian, and Manaen, foster-brother of Herod the tetrarch, and Saul. And as they were ministering to the Lord and fasting, the Holy Spirit said, Separate me now Barnabas and Saul for the work to which I have called them. Then, having fasted and prayed, and having laid their hands on them, they let them go. They therefore, having been sent forth by the Holy Spirit, went down to Seleucia, and thence sailed away to Cyprus.

Of the four classes of ministers in Ephesians 4, two of them are both local and universal: prophets and teachers. Probably, they begin as local ministry and then develop into universal ministry. We'll look at that as we go on, but either way we see there are people who are called especially into the ministry of the word of God to build up the church.

The church in Antioch had a marvelous beginning. It was entirely different from Jerusalem. In Acts chapter 9, because of the persecution in Jerusalem, the disciples who came from Hellenistic countries began to go back to their homelands. As they went back, they brought the gospel of Jesus Christ to their home cities. They traveled through Phoenicia, Syria, and Antioch. In Antioch there were some Greek proselytes who were converted in Jerusalem. These believers began to speak to their own people, who were Greeks. So the Lord began to work mightily and many Gentiles were converted.

News came to Jerusalem, as we already mentioned. Fortunately, God had already opened the door of the gospel to the Gentiles through the apostle Peter. It had already happened, so the prejudice of the Jews against Gentiles was not as strong anymore. When they heard that the Lord was saving those Gentiles in Antioch, they wanted to have some fellowship with them. Not in the sense of Jerusalem acting as the mother church and trying to bring Antioch under their influence—not at all. They wanted to have fellowship. They wanted to know what the Lord was doing in other places. O brothers and sisters, it is something most edifying and profitable to know what God is doing in other parts of the world. For God is not just limited to us here. He is a big God. He is working all over this world. And to know what God is working really enriches the people of God. So the church in Jerusalem wanted to have some fellowship, some contact with the church in Antioch.

15—Local Ministry of the Word

Sending out apostles from Jerusalem would seem too official, it would look suspicious of trying to bring Antioch under Jerusalem; so they sent out Barnabas, the son of consolation. He went there and saw what God was doing and was so encouraged. He exhorted them to continue on following the Lord. And the Lord continued to add and Barnabas began to realize the work was too much for him. He then remembered Saul of Tarsus. So he went to Cilicia and found Saul and brought him back to Antioch. Then the two of them ministered the word of God to the people in Antioch for a whole year. No wonder that church was built by the solid word of God, and the disciples were called Christians for the first time in Antioch.

This reminds me of a similar story. I remember during the wartime, the Lord brought my wife and I out of Singapore and by the providence of God, we arrived in Madras, India. It was one year earlier, there in Madras, that God started a work through brother Bakht Singh. You know dear brother Bakht Singh? Some of you may know him. Dear brother Bakht Singh was saved in Canada. He received his college degree and felt God call him back to India to preach the gospel. So he went home and began to preach the gospel and many people were saved. He traveled all over India preaching the gospel; yet when he returned to the cities where he had preached, he found that many of the new believers were nowhere to be found. The so-called churches in these cities were not able to take care of them spiritually. These traditional churches were not living and he didn't know what to do. So after several years, he was so perplexed. And at one time he went to a hill to wait upon the Lord to see what the Lord would have him do. There were two brothers from England, an elderly lady from England, and Bakht Singh—four of them. They prayed every morning for two months. Just prayed, seeking the Lord. And as they spoke of this to the Lord, God revealed to Bakht Singh what he should do. So he went down from the hill. He went to Madras and there he started the work.

When the work started, these two brothers from England, were young at that time, but no longer are now. I know them all. They were with these brothers in India for a whole year. They had two meetings a day: Before people went to work, they came to listen to the word of God. And after they finished work they came back and listened to the word of God. They met twice a day for a whole year. I visited them during the wartime and half of the people had already left the city since it was shut down. But there were still about two hundred people there. They went down out on the street every day to preach the gospel. By the ministry of the word the church was strengthened. What a testimony!

In the same way that church in Antioch must have been so strengthened by the ministry of the word. They were first called Christians, which means

15—Local Ministry of the Word

Christ's men—ones who are Christ centered. Christ was all to them. And not only did they have that testimony, but through the years God began to raise up some other people into that local ministry of the word. In Acts 13 there were five prophets and teachers. Barnabas, Simeon, Lucius, Manaen and Saul. These five prophets and teachers were not elders of the church in Antioch. Their main work was to minister the word of God to the church in Antioch. And we see in them the most beautiful things. We do not find them ministering to the house of God. Instead, they were ministering to the Lord. Only then can they minister to the house of God, the hearts of people. Unless one ministers to the Lord first, their ministry to the people will not be effective. So here these five were ministering unto the Lord. Waiting upon the Lord. Trying to receive the mind of the Lord. Trying to know what the Lord wants to say to His people. Now as they were waiting there together the Spirit of God said, "Set apart for Me, Barnabas and Saul for the work that I sent them to do."

In the church in Antioch, these five prophets and teachers actually represent the local ministry. They were ministering to the local church in Antioch. And out of that, God set apart two to do the apostolic work. Notice it is from the church that apostles are developed. First of all, you find that these five were ministering to the local church, not to the church universal. But as they ministered to the local church,

God sent two prophets and teachers out to minister to the church universal. We do not find the other three traveling to different cities and ministering the word of God.

Let us look more closely at these five who were ministering the word together there in Antioch. As to Barnabas, what is possibly his gift? He was called "the son of consolation" (Acts 4:36). In other words, he would exhort and encourage the believers. So most likely his gift was a teaching gift.

We know something else about Barnabas. If you go back to Acts chapter 4, at that time those who believed in the Lord, gathered together in one accord in Jerusalem. How they loved one another! How they cared for one another! What a testimony they had. And there were many needs in the church in Jerusalem. During the Pentecost festival, at the beginning of the church, there were lots of Jews saved from all over the world. These did not go back to their homes but stayed in Jerusalem. Because of that, there were tremendous physical needs. Barnabas' Jewish name was Joseph, he was a Cyprian, a Hellenistic Jew, and a Levite. He sold his possessions in Jerusalem and laid the money at the feet of the apostles to support the widows and people in need. That was Barnabas. They called him Barnabas—the apostles gave him that name which means "the son of consolation." They called him this because he was used of God to console, to comfort, to help many brothers and sisters.

15—Local Ministry of the Word

In other words, we see his being a shepherd is manifested while he was in Jerusalem. And then later in Antioch he was ministering as a teacher there.

The second one mentioned was Simeon who was called Niger. We do not know his background. We only know he was called Niger, which means black. He may have come from Africa. But there in Antioch he was raised up by God as a prophet or as a teacher. He was ministering there.

And there was Lucius the Cyrenian. Possibly one of the first to preach the gospel there in Antioch (Acts 11:19-20).

And there was Manaen, the foster-brother of Herod the Tetrach. He must come from a very noble family.

Finally we find Saul, who was later called Paul. What is the gift of the apostle Paul? We say apostle is an office, a commission, but an apostle must have gifts. And if we read the word of God we may be able to discover what his gifting was. In II Timothy 1:11 Paul says of himself, "I was appointed a herald and an apostle and a teacher." So probably his gift is a teaching gift. Then in Ephesians 3 he mentions he has received revelation to know the mystery of the Christ. So he may be a prophet, too. He may have had both the gift of teaching and the gift of prophesying.

These five came from very different backgrounds. God brought them to Antioch having different ethnicities, different upbringings, and yet they served together as one. It was very beautiful. And through their ministry, the church in Antioch grew continuously.

16—How Local Ministry Develops

II Timothy 3:14-17—But thou, abide in those things which thou hast learned, and of which thou hast been fully persuaded, knowing of whom thou hast learned them; and that from a child thou hast known the sacred letters, which are able to make thee wise unto salvation, through faith which is in Christ Jesus. Every scripture is divinely inspired, and profitable for teaching, for conviction, for correction, for instruction in righteousness; that the man of God may be complete, fully fitted to every good work.

How does ministry in the local church evolve? We acknowledge that there is tremendous need today in local assemblies everywhere for the ministry of God's word. But we would like to know how it evolves. In the case in Antioch, at least we know the history of two of them. So, let's use these two as examples.

Barnabas

We know some of the history of Barnabas. Barnabas was a Levite; and being born a Levite he was supposed to serve in the temple in Jerusalem.

Therefore, from his childhood, he must have been trained for such service. He must have been acquainted with temple service, and all of the Old Testament Scriptures—the Torah, the prophets, and the Psalms—because he was trained for that purpose. He had that background. We do not know whether he was one among the 3,000 who were saved on the day of Pentecost. Probably he was. After he believed in the Lord Jesus, with his new light and new life, his understanding of the word of God greatly increased. He was able to use the word of God to comfort, to exhort, to encourage God's people.

Even before Barnabas was saved, God had already prepared him. Even before we are born (Isaiah 49:1-2); as a matter of fact, even before the foundation of the world, we were already chosen in Christ Jesus (Ephesians 1:4). Even when we were in the mother's womb, God had already set us apart (Galatians 1:15, Jeremiah 1:5). In other words, even all the days and years before we were saved, everything that happened in our lives—we did not know, but God knew—He was preparing us for something of His will. Then after we were saved, what God had prepared beforehand began to be manifested. It is true that all the past had to go through death and resurrection before God could use us, but the preparation was already in place.

Moses is a good example of this. God's hand was on Moses as a little baby. God preserved his life. And God put him in the palace to learn all the learnings of

16—How Local Ministry Develops

Egypt. He was mighty in words and deeds (Acts 7:22). When he was forty he thought, "Now it is time for me to go look after my brethren—the Hebrews—to help them, to deliver them, to save them." And he tried to use his speech and his fists to save his own brethren; and was rejected. So, he had to flee for his life. It then took another forty years in the wilderness to unlearn everything that he had learned in Egypt. When he was eighty, he said, "I cannot speak." And that was true! "Who am I to go to see Pharaoh?" He was no longer that great man.

But dear brothers and sisters even so, what happened during those forty years was not lost. It went to death and resurrection and God used him. For a man to lead two million people who were not organized, a motley group of people—two million men, women, children and mixed multitudes—and he led them for forty years in the wilderness. If he did not have that kind of training in the palace of Egypt to govern the greatest empire in the world at that time he would not be able to do it. He had been preparing to govern the greatest empire in the world; but of course, all of this training had to go through death and resurrection.

So, whatever God has given you, even before you were saved, is for God's use; but it has to go through death and resurrection. Why? Otherwise you will use it for your own glory. And you will do disservice to

God instead of service to God. With Barnabas God had already prepared a vessel for His purpose.

Saul

We also know a little about Saul's background. Saul of Tarsus. He was trained in Jerusalem under the feet of Gamaliel—the greatest rabbi at that time (Acts 22:3). And Saul became a Pharisee. A Pharisee of the Pharisees. He knew the Old Testament by heart. But, unfortunately, he was blinded by Jewish tradition; and thought Jesus was an imposter. He put all of his natural strength in persecuting and wiping out the followers of Jesus. Then the Lord met him on the road to Damascus. Immediately his whole being was turned around. His eyes were opened and he was baptized. He began to preach that Jesus is the Christ; the one whom he persecuted was the Messiah (Acts 9).

Between verse 21 and 22 of Acts chapter 9 was a time period of about three years of Paul's life unrecorded in the book of Acts but mentioned in Galatians 1.* When Paul was first saved on the road to Damascus, immediately he began to proclaim that Jesus is the Son of God. Why? Because he had personally met Him. He knew from his own

---

* For more details on the chronology of events in Paul's early stage of Christian life see *God Has Spoken in Galatians: Seeing Christ through Errors* by Stephen Kaung.

16—How Local Ministry Develops

experience that Jesus is the Son of God (Acts 9:20). Then he left Damascus and spent about three years in Arabia in the desert (Galatians 1:17-18). We do not know whether he went to Mount Sinai or not. Probably, yes. Why? Because he had to restudy the word of God with the light of the Lord Jesus. He already knew the Old Testament by heart; but didn't have the right light. In the past he read it all wrong. Now he had to go back and spend about three years alone before God and let the Holy Spirit teach him anew of Christ Jesus in the word of God.

After three years he returned to Damascus and then he began to argue with people that "Jesus is the Christ. I know it," and he proved it from the Old Testament scriptures. He got too hot and he had to be let down by basket over the wall and fled. And he went to Jerusalem (Acts 9:22-25).

But he had a very bad name in Jerusalem among the believers because he had persecuted them before he was a Christian. So nobody dared to be in touch with him. He wanted to find the believers. He wanted to have fellowship. He knew that he couldn't be alone. He wanted to be with the brothers and sisters but nobody dared to touch him. Barnabas, however, had a big heart. He believed in him. He brought him to the apostles and Paul began to go in and out with the disciples. And he began again to argue with the people about the Lord Jesus; and again he began to be too hot to handle. So finally, the brothers in Jerusalem had to send him away, because he became too hot even for them to handle. They sent him back to Tarsus.

What did he do there? If you read Galatians you know while he was in Tarsus for several years there, he was not idle. There he was traveling in Cilicia and Syria, preaching Jesus Christ. And people in Jerusalem and Judea had never seen him, but they had heard about him. They heard he was very zealous for the Lord, preaching Christ Jesus in Cilicia and in Syria. As a matter of fact, he was very difficult to find in Syria. When Barnabas tried to go to Tarsus to find him, he had to search for him, because he traveled so fast. And Barnabas caught up with him and brought him to Antioch. God had been preparing him all along.

Timothy

Timothy is another good illustration. You'll find that when Barnabas and Paul went to Galatia's cities to preach the gospel, they went to Lystra where Timothy was; and God did a miracle there which most likely was the time of Timothy's salvation. Because of the miracle, the people in the city thought that he and Barnabas were Zeus and Mercury. They wanted to offer bulls to them in worship. Paul and Barnabas rent their clothes and jumped into their midst saying "Don't do that! That's what we are trying to tell you not to do, because we are telling you about

16—How Local Ministry Develops

the true living God." It was difficult for them to keep the crowds from sacrificing to them. Then some Jews from Antioch and Iconium came and persuaded the crowds to turn on them. They stopped trying to worship and instead stoned Paul until they thought he was dead. Most likely he was dead. They dragged him out of the city Lystra and dropped him there. And the disciples were surrounding him assuming he was dead, but Paul stood up and went back into the city with them (Acts 14:1-20). Now we do not know whether it was that time that he referred to in II Corinthians when he said "I know a man in Christ, who fourteen years ago was taken up to the third heaven. Who was taken away to paradise and heard things that no one can utter" (12:2-4). We do not know whether it was at that time or not. But, anyway, you'll find Timothy was saved in Lystra during that time.

But Timothy had a good background. His father was a Greek; his mother was a Jew. She was in the Hellenistic background which is not as strict as those in Israel; so his mother married a Greek Gentile (Acts 16:1). Now the grandmother, Lois, and the mother, Eunice, actually were very God-fearing (II Timothy 1:5). And some people think that probably they were among those first disciples converted on the day of Pentecost in Jerusalem. We don't know. But, anyway, they brought up that little boy with the word of God. They nurtured him with the sacred letter. But he was not saved until Paul went there to Lystra and preached the word. Then Timothy was saved, born again. So Paul considered Timothy as his son (I Timothy 1:2).

This Timothy was a young man or a lad. And Timothy began to meet with these brothers and sisters in Lystra. This young man had a tremendous knowledge of the sacred letter. He had that background. And because he loved the Lord he sought the Lord, and the Lord gave him understanding. Even though he was a young man, yet he began to minister the word of God to the brethren in Lystra. Not only in Lystra, but even in Iconium.

Brothers and sisters, the local church is the place of training for the ministry of God's word. The local church should provide opportunity for those who are exercised towards the ministry of the word, to give them opportunity to develop. Some may be called to minister the word, some may not; but the local church is the training ground. Thank God for the local church in Lystra. They did not look upon that young man and despise him; but gave him opportunity. Eventually, they recommended him highly to Paul. And Paul and Silas took him on their missionary journey (Acts 16:1-3). That's how Timothy was developed.

17—Our Need for Local Ministry

II Timothy 4:2, 5—I testify before God and Christ Jesus, who is about to judge living and dead, and by his appearing and his kingdom, proclaim the word; be urgent in season and out of season, convict, rebuke, encourage, with all longsuffering and doctrine.

... But thou, be sober in all things, bear evils, do the work of an evangelist, fill up the full measure of thy ministry.

Consider now this matter in your current local assembly setting. Do you sense the need for the ministry of God's word where you gather? And what are you looking for? Are you searching the horizon; looking for some outside help? Are you hoping that God will send some people from outside to minister the word of God to you? Is that what you're looking for? Well, I do not say that you should close your doors to all ministry from outside. You never want to shut the door against the apostles, prophets, evangelists and teachers. But if you think that the ministry of God's word *must* come from outside help, you are very wrong. You are looking in the wrong direction. Outside ministry is helpful, but it is like having a feast—once in a while it is a blessing, but if you have a feast every day for every meal, you will spoil your stomach. It will make you sick. You want to have a feast if you have not had one for a long time; but if you have a feast day in and day out you grow tired of it. You would rather have some congee, if you know what congee is—watery rice. Brothers and sisters, in our daily life, we need to eat simple food. We cannot live on feasts. But once in a while we need a feast. Now that's what outside ministry is for.

Furthermore, there is a potential problem with outside ministry. I'm not talking about those who proclaim themselves as apostles, as prophets, as teachers, as evangelists. We have plenty of false ministers of the word today. And they will come and say "I am a prophet. I've come to set you in order." "I am a prophet. I'm going to tell you what you should do." "I am a teacher; I am going to teach you some very deep doctrine—that very few people know." "I'm coming to take over your life." No, I'm not talking about these people. I'm talking about true prophets, true teachers, true apostles, true evangelists. True servants of God. Even though these true ministers of the word of God have a message, they do not know your local conditions. They will come and share their burden with you. Sometimes they may overburden you, because you are not ready for it. Sometimes those preachers may burden the believers with something too mature, that the Spirit of God hasn't yet lead them into. And as the saints try to follow that ministry they

17—Our Need for Local Ministry

may be damaged. Brothers and sisters, this is the danger. They do not know the local conditions. They are not able to supply the local need.

A shepherd knows his sheep (John 10:14). He knows what kind of pasture his sheep need at this particular moment. But someone coming from outside, even with great gifting, will not know the local situation. They may pour upon you something that is not your need at this moment. Consider these poor brothers and sisters. When one brother comes with a tremendous message, they are swayed to the east for a moment. Then after a few days another one comes with a very strong message and they sway to the west. They are tossed and swayed around. This is a problem sometimes with outside ministry. Fortunately, some who visit local assemblies really have waited upon the Lord. Instead of just sharing their burden, they try to find from the Lord His burden for a specific locality. But I'm afraid it's very rare. Today, most who are traveling around just carry some messages in their heart and no matter who they share with, they give the same message. It is like giving aspirin for every sickness.

Do you think the Lord, who loves the church so much and gave His own life for her, who nourishes her, and cherishes her, will not provide the ministry of the word for her? What is nourishing? Nourishing is providing for all the food that she needs. Do you think that the Head of the body, the Lord who loves His church so much, has made no provision for you? Do you think He does not cherish you? He does not nourish you? Can you believe that? I cannot.

Some think, "Well, what should we do with the ministry of the word? If God sends in someone, or even if someone is raised up here, who will take over the ministry when they leave?" In other words, they think they need a hired Pastor. Now, brothers and sisters, the only place where we can find the word *pastor* in the New Testament is in Ephesians 4:11-12 "pastors and teachers." This word pastor, in all the other places in the New Testament, is not translated *pastor but shepherd*. Only in Ephesians 4 the translators translated it *pastor*. Actually in the original language, it is *shepherd—shepherds* and teachers. There is no pastor in the New Testament. Why do they translate this as *pastor*? It is because the pastor system is the tradition of the translators. So, in this instance, they translate shepherd as pastor. Remember: the pastor system is not in the Scripture. The pastor or shepherd is a gift in the scripture. We thank God for giving His church shepherds/pastors and teachers.

As a matter of fact, pastors and teachers are one person, not two. They are both aspects of one who deals with the word of God. One is teaching publicly—teachers; the other is counseling privately—shepherds. That's shepherding. You know, all the elders in the church shepherd the flock of God (I Peter 5:1-2). They are all shepherds. They counsel,

17—Our Need for Local Ministry

they help, and some of the elders may have teaching ministry publicly, but not all.

So, today people try to fill in their local lack in the ministry of the word. And they look for someone who will come and take over the ministry. And, sure enough, Christianity has developed a way to supply that provision. It is not the Head who provides pastors; it is Christianity that provides them with a Pastor. Why? Because they send people to seminary, train them with the skill, and then ordain them. They then employ them as the Pastor. Those trained Pastors will try to take care of all the spiritual needs of the church. They will minister the word of God and counsel. They not only do the work of ministering the word of God, they go back like in the early days in Jerusalem with the apostles waiting on tables; they seem to do everything for the congregation. It is as if no one needs to do anything—just sit there, let the pastor do the work. That is the pastoral system which Christianity has developed. How contradictory it is to the very principle that is the life of the church!

Brothers and sisters, are you looking for a pastor to come and take care of you? Is this the way of God? No. Can you believe that if the Lord gathers you together around Him as a local expression of the church that He will not take care of you? Can you believe?—are you able to look up to Him for the supply and raise up among you brothers who are able to minister the word of God? Do you have that faith?

I'm afraid it's because we do not have that faith, that we do not have local ministry of the word. If we have the faith and we look up to the Lord, no doubt He will raise up some among us who will be able to minister the word of God. Maybe not as good as Paul, maybe not as good as Timothy, but it is good enough for us.

How does God raise up these people? Some of you may have a so-called Christian background. You may be brought up in a Christian family. You may have gone to Sunday school. Or you may even have attended a mission school for your education or Christian college or whatever it may be. I'm not saying these things are sufficient, not at all, but in God's providence, He has put you in a Christian family. He has given you the opportunity to have contact with the word of God. You may memorize some verses because of some reward as a kid, that's all right. But, anyway, you find that before you believe in the Lord Jesus you already have some background like Timothy, like Paul, like Barnabas. Then one day, the Lord saved you.

Now if you really love the Lord, you will love His word. You will begin to respond to the word of God. In the past you had some knowledge of the word of God, but this was dead knowledge. It did not do you any good, and you really did not understand. It did not speak to your heart; it was only in your mind. But after you were saved, you love the word of God. You begin

17—Our Need for Local Ministry

to spend time with the word before God. You read it daily and meditate upon it. You seek to know the word from Him. And the Holy Spirit begins to open up the word of God to you. Brothers and sisters, this is the way it should be.

And when God's people are together we all try to share whatever the Lord has shown us. And when we begin to share what the Lord is teaching us, we discover the anointing of the Lord is upon someone and brothers and sisters receive help. They are helped and because of this we encourage that particular one to share more. Gradually that teaching ministry or prophetic ministry begins to be developed. That's the way it is developed.

Today, in an organized church, there is not usually an opportunity for people to be trained or developed since someone already has monopolized the ministry. If they notice you developing in ministry the Pastor may be jealous of you, thinking that you are going to take his place.

Brothers and sisters, be very simple with the local ministry of the word. Do not expect that there will be a Paul coming out in your midst. Be very simple, because that's what you need. People may come and give you a tremendous teaching, but it may be all over your head. What is the use of it? God knows what you need today and He is providing for your nourishment. Maybe what you need today is just a simple vegetable dish and that is what you have. Oh brothers and sisters, if you are open to the Lord, if you are open to one another, then you'll find it is almost natural that God will raise up some in your midst who are able to supply the need.

What if there are none among us who come from a so-called Christian background, then what happens? Well, that's even better. They do not need to unlearn what they learned before. God can start with a clean slate if one loves the Lord and has no background of the word of God. With no background there are also no preconceived ideas. Many who read the Bible today are filled in their mind with some interpretations of the word from their tradition. They think they know what the word says, but they don't. But if you know that you don't know, well, you will know. Why? Because you open the word of God and read it and study it and meditate on it before the Lord. You look to the Holy Spirit to teach you—and my what a teacher He is!

So, again, the development is the same. Brothers and sisters are gathered together and each shares what the Lord has given. Gradually the gift is manifested. Some people need to be encouraged to do more; other people need to be discouraged not to do too much. God may not use someone as a prophet or a teacher. But everyone can exhort, encourage and counsel. Everybody can do that, but not all are called to minister the word of God.

17—Our Need for Local Ministry

So the local ministry of the word is very simple. It is therefore neither all-men's ministry nor a one-man's ministry. We can tend to go to two extremes. One extreme is in thinking that we need one person to minister the word of God to us. Now if we have only a one man's ministry, what will we have? If that man only has dessert to give to eat then we have dessert every time. We will not have a well-rounded nourishment of the word of God.

But neither should we go to the other extreme—an all-men ministry thinking that every brother and sister can minister the word of God. No. The word of God is too holy, too sacred for us to handle it with carelessness. Sometimes we may exhort people with the word. But only when the Holy Spirit really gives us that word. But to be involved in local ministry, it demands much more.

This is very simple and in the next chapters we will see how simple it is.

> Dear Lord, You love the church. You gave Yourself for her. You cherished her and nourished her. You have not left us as orphans. You are with us. Lord, give us faith to believe that You do supply every need that we have. We look to Thee. We do not look to the east or the west. We look to Thee. In these last days, we pray that Thou will open the door, open the way for local ministry to be raised up. That the need of Thy people everywhere will

be met. Oh how we praise and thank Thee. We know that this is Thy Will. We know that Thou hast provided. But Lord, we ask that Thou will remove all the obstacles in our midst and let local ministry come up. We ask in the name of our Lord Jesus, amen.

Part Four: The Minister of the Word

18 — The Minister's Attitude

Isaiah 66:2b—But to this man will I look: to the afflicted and contrite in spirit, and who trembleth at my word.

Last time we asked the question: What is local ministry? True, it is the will of God that all the members of the body of Christ function and minister to one another—we need to minister Christ to one another, so that the body may be increased with the increase of God (Ephesians 4:16)—however, our discussion on local ministry is limited specifically to the ministry of the word of God in local assemblies. Every brother and sister can exhort, encourage and comfort (I Corinthians 14:3), but not everyone can minister the word of God in the local assembly. This local ministry of the word is what we are considering, and now we would like to consider how to minister the word of God.

To minister the word of God is a great honor; but it is also a tremendous responsibility. Oftentimes we all only think of the honor—"Oh if I can minister the word of God to His people, that would be wonderful!" But we forget that it is a tremendous responsibility. We consider it as a great honor. Why? Because when we think about how our God is such a holy God, glorious, He who lives in the light, perfect—and yet, He uses men such as we are to speak for Him. And who are we? We are sinners saved by grace. We are imperfect. We are weak. We have defilement, have been corrupted, our lips are unclean, our hearts are deceitful above all things. And yet God condescends himself to choose us to be His mouthpiece. This is almost unthinkable that God should use men to speak for Him. What an honor this is! And yet, with the honor comes a great responsibility. Knowing ourselves and our depravity, we realize how easy it is for us to misrepresent God, to corrupt the word of God, to misunderstand His thoughts, to lower His standard, to twist His words—distorting them to suit our tastes, and for us to limit His words because of our limitations. So, while you think of these things, brothers and sisters, you will feel such a responsibility.

Now, what is the ministry of God's word? Do you merely do some research in the Scriptures like you would research other books? And then try to analyze your research and put your notes in some format to present to the believers? Is that the ministry of God's word? No. The ministry of the word of God is to impart Christ to people through the word. It is not just getting the word out, but in getting out the word you impart Christ to others.

We are "ministers of the new covenant; not of letter, but of spirit. For the letter kills, but the Spirit quickens" (II Corinthians 3:6). If we minister the

18—The Minister's Attitude

word of God just in letter, it will become law to the hearers and it will kill them. But if we minister the word of God in spirit and in deliverance, it sets people free. The ministry of God's word is life unto life, but to certain people it is death unto death (II Corinthians 2:16). It is a matter of life and death. A matter of eternal life and eternal death.

When you understand what the ministry of God's word is, you immediately realize the tremendous responsibility there. Who is competent? Who is adequate to minister God's word? No wonder you find the apostle Paul said, "having this ministry, as we have had mercy shewn us, we faint not" (II Corinthians 4:1). When you really see what the ministry of God's word is it makes you faint, because you know that you are not able to do it. You cannot give life. You do not want to deliver death. How can you impart Christ to people? It is not just speaking some words out loud? This ministry is beyond what anyone can do. Even the apostle Paul said he did not faint because of the mercy of God. This ministry of God's word is a tremendous responsibility. We just cannot touch it very lightly and carelessly. We need to have a certain attitude when we approach God's word.

We mentioned already that God's word is God's work. If you see the work of God in this world, and you remove His word, then there is no work. When you touch God's word you are touching God himself. Therefore, before we can think about how to minister

God's word, we need to have a proper attitude towards God's word.

What is our attitude when we touch God's word? In Isaiah chapter 66 God said, "to this man will I look: to the afflicted and contrite in spirit, and who trembleth at my word" (v.2). When we come to the word of God, we need to have this attitude. We need to have the right spirit. We come to God with an afflicted and contrite spirit. You do not come to the word of God with a proud, lofty, haughty spirit. You come in humility, because you are coming to the word of God and you tremble at His word.

I am afraid today people treat God's word so lightly. They read God's words as if they are reading a history book or worse a fiction novel. We do not have the right attitude when we approach God's word. And because of this, we do not know God's word. God's word will not reveal God's will to us if that is the attitude we have. But when we come to His word with a contrite spirit, and with fear and trembling, then we may discover His will.

It is true that on the one hand we do come to Him with boldness. Just like Hebrews chapter 10 says: "let us approach with a true heart, in full assurance [boldness] of faith" (v.22a-b). Why? Because of the blood of our Lord Jesus. Because of the living way that He has opened for us knowing that He is a high priest interceding for us (vv.21, 22c-d). On such a ground we can come to God with holy boldness. That is true.

18—The Minister's Attitude

But at the same time, that boldness does not mean that we are so bold that we become careless. We know who He is. We know what His word is. We come with fear and trembling, lest we mistreat His word or misunderstand His word. We approach His word with the proper attitude lest due to our weakness we somehow weaken the word of God. Lest we try to bring it down to our level instead of letting it lift us up to His level.

Brothers and sisters, what is our attitude when we come to the word of God? Let us approach it with fear and trembling. With this right mindset we are now able to learn how to minister God's word.

19—The Minister is in the Ministry

I Timothy 4:16a—Take heed to thyself, and to thy teaching (ASV).

In this matter of God's work and the ministry of the word, God always places more emphasis on the person than the work. The apostle Paul said to Timothy, "Take heed to thyself and to thy teaching" (I Timothy 4:16a ASV). The teaching is important because when you are ministering the word of God you are teaching the word of God. But the apostle Paul said to take heed to *yourself* and the teaching. You are more important than what you are going to teach. Why? Because the type of person you are will produce the kind of teaching you teach.

To the pure everything is pure. To the defiled everything is defiled—even his conscience is defiled (see Titus 1:15). So when we approach the word of God, we as a person must be right. If we are not right with God, then when we approach the word of God we will not be able to understand it. Or, as some have said, they do not want to touch God's word because whatever they read speaks to them saying, "You are wrong." It is as if the word of God is scourging them all the time. And because of that they dare not touch God's word. Why? It is because of what they are. The kind of person you are will define the kind of word you read. When you touch the word of God it is important that you are the right kind of person. God always emphasizes more on us than what we do for him. Unfortunately, in this world and in the Christian world, it seems that what we *do* is more important than what we *are*. This is really the very opposite from what God is looking for; He is looking for what we are more than what we do.

> Therefore, having this ministry, as we have had mercy shewn us, we faint not. But we have rejected the hidden things of shame, not walking in deceit, nor falsifying the word of God, but by manifestation of the truth commending ourselves to every conscience of men before God. But if also our gospel is veiled, it is veiled in those that are lost; in whom the god of this world has blinded the thoughts of the unbelieving, so that the radiancy of the glad tidings of the glory of the Christ, who is the image of God, should not shine forth for them. For we do not preach ourselves, but Christ Jesus Lord, and ourselves your bondmen for Jesus' sake (II Corinthians 4:1-5).

we have rejected the hidden things of shame

When the apostle Paul considered this matter of the ministering of the word of God, he said "having

19—The Minister is in the Ministry

this ministry because we have received mercy we faint not. But we have rejected the hidden things of shame." Now, do not think that since you have a certain understanding of God's word, therefore, you can deliver His word despite what you are. Paul basically said, "In order to minister God's word, we reject the hidden things of shame in our lives." What are the hidden things of shame? Is there something in our lives that we feel ashamed of? Is there something we would not like people to know about, and because of that we hide them? Are there things that are questionable in our lives; things that we know is not quite right; or even things that we know is wrong? When there are things that we ourselves are ashamed of, we don't like people to know about them, so we hide them. Are there such things in our lives? If there are, then it will greatly affect your ministering of God's word. You may even say the right word, but you are the wrong person. And the Holy Spirit will not bear witness to what you deliver. There is no life nor power there.

And Paul said you must reject the hidden things of shame in your lives. The word reject is a strong word. It is not that if you are able to hide some shameful thing from others you keep it hidden and therefore it is all right. No, you have to reject them, cast them away, deal with them. Then as you stand before God's people in delivering His word, you can be transparent. You are not afraid to let people look into your lives. If we have things of shame and we hide them, we are hypocrites. We live two lives—one before men and one before God. One in the public and one in private. If that's the case, we are not qualified to deliver God's word.

When our Lord Jesus was on Earth, He was very strict. He denounced the hypocrites. He said, "Woe to you hypocrites!" (see Matthew 23:13) Our Lord is so loving. The little children love to flock to Him. He is so loving that He will not refuse a sinner. And yet the one person that He denounced so strongly was a hypocrite. One who has two faces. One who lives two lives: one in public and one in private. That is what the Lord hates.

not walking in deceit

Look at the life of our Lord Jesus Christ while He was on Earth. He was transparent. He lived only one life. His life before God was the same life as before men. His life by himself alone was the same life that He lived among people. He was an open book, not only before God but also before men. Actually, before God even if you close the book it is always open, but before men you can close your book. The Lord Jesus was transparent, truthful. Even His enemies realized that. They said, "You are true. There is no falsehood in You" (see Matthew 22:16) Why? Because He is the Word. He is the Word became flesh.

19—The Minister is in the Ministry

So in ministering the word of God, it demands us to reject everything of shame in our lives. We must not walk in deceit. If we have anything hidden that we are ashamed of we know those things are not right. We know we are walking in deceit. We have to pretend. We have to put on a façade. We are not being truthful.

And worse than this, walking in deceit also means that we may have some ulterior motive in our hearts. When we are ministering the word of God, we may be trying to get something for ourselves. Either looking for some recognition, "See this brother! How he knows the word of God!" Or, we may be ambitious. There might be some ulterior motive in us, some gain for our personal reasons. That is what happens when we are walking deceitfully. Those who minister the word of God must not walk deceitfully. Our motives must be searched by the light of God, that we have no other motive than to do the will of God. No other motive than to fulfill what the Lord has called us to do. No other motive, but to build the church.

nor falsifying the word of God

Nor can we falsify the word of God. It is easy for us to falsify the word of God—to adulterate the word of God, to distort the word of God, to change the word of God to suit our needs, our taste, or to please the hearers. If we do that then we are not cutting the word of God in a straight line (see II Timothy 2:15).

Oftentimes when administering the word of God we are tempted to compromise His word. Why? Because we want to please our hearers. If we deliver God's word as we are given it by Him then we are afraid that people may reject us. People may not be pleased or happy with us. In order to get their approval we may falsify the word.

Falsify does not mean that you change it completely. You may change it a little bit or you may add a little bit. Even in the Garden of Eden, when Satan came and tempted Eve, Eve's dialogue with Satan was falsifying the word of God. Satan said, "Did God say you cannot eat from any tree in the garden?" What an insinuation! At that time man lived by the fruit of the trees. And God provided all these trees and the fruits for men to eat. Satan dared to suggest God said they could not eat any fruit from any tree. In other words, he was saying, "God is so cruel. He wants to starve you to death. He doesn't love you." Satan was falsifying the word of God. Then Eve returned by falsifying the word of God in another way saying, "No, no, no. God said you cannot eat only this tree—the tree of the knowledge of good and evil—He said we cannot even touch it." That was falsifying God's word since He had not said anything about touching it or not.

In various ministry within Christianity today the word of God is falsified, adulterated in order to suit the itching ears of men or in order to gain selfishly

19—The Minister is in the Ministry

from the ministry. They do not cut the word of God in a straight line. If this is your way, you are disqualified to speak the word of God.

by manifestation of the truth

Here it says, "manifestation of the truth." What is the manifestation of the truth? It is twofold. On the one hand, you are able to present the truth as it is without adulterating it—without changing it—without corrupting it. On the other hand, when you are presenting the truth, in a way, you are also the embodiment of the very truth you are presenting to the people. It means that you are not just telling people a truth, but it is true to you as well. It is possible for you to present the truth as a truth, and it really is a truth, but still that truth is not true to you personally. I do not mean that you do not believe it. Some people nowadays do not even believe the word is true. You may present the truth and yet not believe it yourself. Even if you do believe the truth sometimes you cannot manifest it because it is not real to you. You have not experienced it. You do not know the power of that truth in your life.

commending ourselves to every conscience of men before God

Again, the apostle Paul said, "by the manifestation of the truth, commending ourselves to every conscience of men before God." Do you know what preaching is? What teaching is? What ministering the word of God is? It is reaching the conscience and not merely the mind. If you study the Bible mind-to-mind you may go to a seminary, complete study courses, and have a certain understanding of the Bible in your mind. Then when you deliver what you understand and know to the congregation as it comes out of your mind, the only place it can reach is other people's minds. If you share in that way the word cannot reach other people's consciences, since even your own conscience has not been touched.

A lot of preaching today is in the mental realm. It is almost like teaching philosophy or ethics. There is no difference there between the two of them. But what is real ministering of the word? It is from conscience to conscience. Only that which touches the conscience transforms life. If it only touches people's minds it will not change them. You may have your head full of theology, but it won't help your life. Whenever the word of God truly goes forth it touches people's consciences.

On the day of Pentecost, when Peter stood up and the Eleven with him, they preached the resurrection of our Lord Jesus. What happened? Those who listened were pricked in their hearts. In other words, their consciences were touched, not their minds. The resurrection of the Lord Jesus was not just a teaching to them. They were not merely trying to

19—The Minister is in the Ministry

figure out whether or not there was a resurrection. No. When the resurrection of the Lord Jesus was presented to them their consciences were pricked. Why? Because here was One whom they crucified, and now He was raised from the dead. What are they to do now with that Person? That was the manifestation of the truth being commended to every conscience of men before God.

In delivering the word you are actually delivering yourself to people. You cannot deliver God's word without yourself being involved. You are actually giving yourself when you give out the word. And whether or not it can touch people's conscience depends on whether the truth that you present is real to you. That is the ministry of the word of God. We need to mourn for what is happening, especially in this country. It is as if the word of God fills the air everywhere. But where are the consciences being touched? How do we deliver the word of God? This has been taken so lightly by us that we act as if anybody may preach. No, it is a tremendous responsibility.

But if also our gospel is veiled ...

Paul was also even able to say, "if the gospel is veiled, it is veiled in those that are lost because the god of this world has blinded their eyes." In other words, he delivered the word of God in such a way—He discharged His responsibility in such a proper way—

that if anyone did not see it and receive it, the responsibility was in that one and not in Paul. Now, can we say that as he did? Oftentimes after we deliver a message, we find that the message does not seem to touch people. And we know we are partially responsible because we are not what we should be. But Paul can say "if the gospel that I preached is veiled the responsibility is not in me. It is in you. Because your eyes have been blinded by the god of this world. The world has so occupied your mind and your conscience is hardened so much so that the word cannot reach into your heart."

*we do not preach ourselves,
but Christ Jesus Lord*

He said, "We preach Jesus Christ. We do not preach ourselves." And yet in preaching Jesus Christ you have to go out with what we preach. This is the way that we are called to deliver the word of God.

20—Necessities for Ministry

What are the fundamental necessities in delivering the word of God? There are certain fundamental things that the ministers of the word must have in order to truly minister the word.

1—The Minister Must Have Vision

> Where there is no vision the people cast off restraint (Proverbs 29:18a).

First of all, those who minister the word of God need vision. We have been stating this again and again because we feel this is so important. For those in church government, they need vision, because if they do not have vision they are not able to lead God's people. And for those who are in the ministry of the word need vision, because without vision they cannot direct God's people.

"Where there is no vision, the people perish" (KJV). Others have translated it as, "Without vision the people is disintegrate." Or in some versions it is translated "Without vision the people cast off restraint." Vision is an absolute necessity for people who minister the word of God. We have 66 books in the Bible and it touches on so many things. It is so broad. You need vision to know how to handle God's word. Because if you do not have vision, you will see in the word of God a little here a little there—a line here and a line there. And these lines do not connect with each other. You need a vision that will somehow take up all the various parts of word of God and join them into one. Vision is that which gives us a center. The word of God has a center.

Scripture not only has a center but also an outline. The apostle Paul said to Timothy, "Have the outline of sound words" (II Timothy 1:13). There is an outline. There is a scope. It is almost like you have a center and then you have an outer circle or circumference. And there are numberless—countless things in between, but they are all centered upon the center and circumscribed by the outline.

That is the word of God. Not just here a little and there a little. Scriptures are not to be isolated and unrelated or even contradictory to one another. No. But where do you get that ability to bring them all together? That comes with a vision.

When we say vision now we do not mean the same thing as when some people say, "Well, yesterday I saw a vision. I saw something floating in the heavens." We do not mean that. By vision we mean the Spirit of God unveils to us that which is in the heart and mind of God from eternity to eternity. It is not something you see with your eyes. You may, but if you do, you will become blind. Because the light is too big—too strong. Paul on the road to Damascus saw the righteous One but His eyes turned blind. So, by vision we do not mean that you see something with your physical eyes. By vision we mean that God reveals and you see. But you do not see it with your naked eyes you see it in your spirit. The Holy Spirit reveals the mind and heart of God to your spirit. So, deep down in your spirit you saw something. That's vision.

This vision has to do with eternal purpose of God. The purpose that God has purposed in himself even before the foundation of the world (Ephesians 1:9-11. It is according to that purpose that God has been working throughout the ages and the centuries (3:11). And is that which God will have in the eternity to come. That vision concerns this eternal purpose of God. The whole Bible is to reveal that purpose. That heart and mind of God, we call this the eternal word (Psalm 119:89). God's truth is eternal, everlasting, because it is from eternity to eternity (Isaiah 43:13). But you need to see it.

Even in this world, if we use this concept in a more broad way, if you want to do anything you need a vision or a dream. As Martin Luther King Jr. said, "I have a dream!" Why? Because without a vision, you have no goal. You have no direction. You do not have that power within you to endure. You will not have that passion within you to give yourself to it. Without vision you will be a victim. You just drift—meaningless—purposeless it is vision that give us purpose—that sets our life in a certain direction. And despite opposition and obstacles, it gives you the strength to press on.

Vision is also that which unites—joins people together. You know people with one vision can work together. If they do not have the same vision, how can they work together? One wants to go one direction, and another wants to go another direction. Is this integration? Without vision the people disintegrate—even perish. It ends up in nothing. Brothers and sisters, you know what is the basic need in the church today? Vision. Why is it that God's people scatter or disintegrate? Because they have different visions. They do not have *the* vision from God.

In the Scripture, you find vision and visions. Even the apostle Paul, at the end of his testifying before King Agrippa said, "King Agrippa, I have not been disobedient to the heavenly vision" (Acts 26:19). Then to the Corinthians he said, Now, I will come to this matter of revelations and visions (II Corinthians 12:1). So, you find there is the vision and many visions. Actually, visions should all be part of the one main vision. Now, unfortunately we may have many visions among God's people but no eternal vision.

It is almost like we are putting together a puzzle. We have a puzzle, but all these different pieces of it are very odd by themselves. As a matter of fact, no piece has any meaning to it. So, we try to make a meaning out of each piece. Now, someone picks up

20—Necessities for Ministry

one piece and that becomes his vision and he tries to make a meaning out of that odd piece and he ends up becoming an odd person. And then another person takes another piece—a different piece. And she says "Now, this is my vision! This is what I see." And sure enough, they each become very strange people. Nothing connects or is related to the others. If instead, they would look at a larger picture of the whole puzzle they would discover just exactly where that smaller piece of the puzzle fits in. The eternal vision unites all of the smaller visions.

Brothers and sisters, some people latch onto one truth in the Bible and make it their center and circumstance. It breaks them apart from others; or worse, they become a cult. We cannot be together with so many visions. Why? Because we have different pieces. And we do not want to be joined together. Some have a vision of doing this. Some have a vision of doing that.

As a matter of fact, nothing really exists or can continue without a uniting vision. Whatever group or fellowship or denomination or system in Christianity, whatever it may be, there must be a vision somewhere. Because without visions they cannot continue. Someone must have had a vision in the beginning, and other people begin to get that vision so they end up together. And that vision enables them to continue on. But unfortunately, sometimes it's not a vision given by God. We have in Christianity today certain sects. They have a vision but are not given by God. I do not want to name these people. You know them all. And other people may have a vision, but it is a limited vision. They do not have the right center. And because of that there is not the outline of the sound word. It's all lopsided and fragmented. How pitiful that because of this God's people are divided.

So we can see how necessary it is for the church to have vision. And those who minister the word of God should be the people who supply that vision. But if you do not have the vision yourself how can you supply it? Paul talks about the heavenly vision. His whole life and ministry was governed by the heavenly vision. It was for that heavenly vision that he gave his all. He said, "I was not disobedient to the heavenly vision. That vision was given to me on the road of Damascus. I saw it, and it transformed my whole life. I got involved with it. Even unto death, I was obedient to that vision." It is a matter of obedience.

What is the vision he saw on the road to Damascus as he was approaching the city? God always allows someone to go only so far. He lets you go just far enough, and then His long cord of love stops you. This is like when a child is still learning to walk, and he tends to walk away. And when you go out, you tie a rope around him and then let him walk as far as the rope lets him. Actually, that is not exactly the way our heavenly Father deals with us. He has a cord of love, and the cord of love is really long. He allows us to go

20—Necessities for Ministry

very far. But when we come to a certain point, He pulls back on the cord out of love for us.

So here was Saul, the Pharisee persecuting the church. The Lord had allowed him to do that, not only in Jerusalem but also in Judea and even other cities. He had already gone very far with it. He found no more people to persecute in Jerusalem. The Christians had hidden from him. He couldn't find them anymore. Probably, they were in the catacombs. He couldn't find them. He couldn't find any even in the area of Judea. They all vanished. So, he got documents of authority from the high priest to go to the Gentile cities to seize those believers and bring them to Jerusalem to persecute them. The Lord had allowed him to do all these things. But then before he reached Damascus—I think probably Damascus was almost in view—the Lord let him go until he was almost there, but he was stopped before he reached it. The light from heaven shone upon him brighter than the midday sun. It was so powerful it broke him and prostrated him on the ground. Then he heard a voice, "Saul, Saul, why do you persecute me? Do you know it is hard for you to kick against the goads?" (Acts 26:14) Somebody in heaven knew him. Knew his name, Saul. Saul was not only famous on Earth; he was famous in heaven, too. "Saul, Saul, why do you persecute me? It is hard for you to kick against the goads? Do you know what you are doing?" Even before Paul was in this situation—even when He was in his mother's womb, God has already set him apart for His purpose (Galatians 1:15). He was known by the Lord, even though he did not know the Lord.

Is this not true with every one of us? God has a purpose on each one of us. But we do not know it. And as a matter of fact, what is life? Why is life given to us? Why are we born? Why are we in this world? God has a purpose. God has a meaning. God has a reason for us to be here. We are to be used by Him for His purpose. The picture here is like a horse or a mule that will be used by God to plow the field so the work of God may be done. The mule is not free. There is someone holding the reigns, and it is not the mule. When we try to control our own life to serve God we end up doing the opposite. Saul, for example, was doing a *dis*service to God, instead of serving Him.

Evidently God had already spoken to him in some way, most likely it began when Stephen was martyred. This young man Saul was watching them stone Stephen as he held the clothes of those who stoned him. He witnessed Stephen crying out: "I saw the heavens open and the Son of God standing there." And he heard Stephen when he was dying: "Lord, forgive them" (Acts 7:55-60). I do believe that when Saul saw this and heard this, his conscience was pricked. He knew he was doing something wrong. He knew it. But his past education—his tradition was so strong in him. He tried to stifle his conscience. So, the Bible says he persecuted even more fiercely (Acts 8:1,

3; 9:1). Why? He wanted to silence his own conscience. God said, "It is hard for you to kick against the goads. You try to go your own way, not the way of God. I have touched you with the pricks—with the goads."

Goads are like a tool with a sharpened end. The farmer uses the goad to just touch the animal when the animal wants to go astray instead of straight. These are not meant to hurt the animal, but simply to remind him who the master is. But Saul was kicking against the goads. So, the Lord said, "it is hard for you to kick against the goads. You will be hurt if you continue that." And Saul said, "Lord, who are you?" He said, "I am Jesus, whom you are persecuting." Saul then capitulated and said, "Lord, what should I do?" In other words, he surrendered his life to the risen Lord. What did he see? What is the heavenly vision that he's talking about? He saw Christ the Head—the Head in heaven. He saw the church is the body of Christ on this Earth.

"Saul, Saul, why do you persecute me?" Saul did not argue and say, "Lord, where—when did I persecute you? You are in heaven. I cannot touch you. I haven't done it." No. He understood. When he touched God's people in Jerusalem, he touched the Head of the church, Christ. When he touched people—God's people in Judea, the body of Christ, he touched the Head. As he's going to Damascus to touch the believers there, he is persecuting the Head.

Brothers and sisters, what a picture. He saw the vision of Christ the Head high above all; and he saw the body of Christ covering the whole Earth. That is the heavenly vision he saw! And he was never disobedient to that vision.

If you see this vision, it gives you the center. The center of God's word is Christ and with him the church His body. It gives you the outline of the word being the Son of God. You'll find everything in the Scripture is centered upon Christ. Every truth comes out of Christ and touches the church as the circumference. I remember many years ago, dear brother Watchman, he told us, he said if you really see Christ in the church, the whole Bible is open to you. How true it is.

So, dear brothers and sisters, we need to go to the Lord to ask Him to reveal Christ and the church to us. And if we had that vision then all these odd pieces of the puzzle will fit together. That's the first absolute need for the ministry of God's word.

2—The Minister Must Know the Word

> ... and that from a child thou hast known the sacred letters, which are able to make thee wise unto salvation, through faith which is in Christ Jesus (II Timothy 3:15).

20—Necessities for Ministry

The second need is to know the sacred letters. Paul said to Timothy "You are well acquainted with the sacred letters from your childhood." In other words, he was brought up with the word of God. To minister the word we need to know the word, that ought to be evident to us.

Unfortunately, today in many pulpits, you really don't need to know the word because you are not talking about the word. You are talking about social or political problems. If you know the world, it is enough. But if you really want to minister the word, you have to know the word of God. You have to read it. You have to memorize it. You have to meditate on it. You have to seek the Lord about it. You have to allow the word to work in your own life. You have to be convicted by the word. You have to be enlarged spiritually by the word—uplifted by the word. You weep over the word. You laugh over the word. Brothers and sisters, you need to be acquainted with the word of God.

When I first came to this country I discovered one thing among the Christians in this country. I hope I am wrong now. I discovered that Christians in this country knew a lot. But all they knew came by hearing sermons and not by reading the Scriptures themselves. They heard a lot, but they did not read the word a lot. And because of this, they could easily be swayed and deceived. There was no sure foundation—solid foundation. All believers need to have a solid foundation of the word of God.

You may read a lot about the word of God, but you do not read the word of God as you should. You read lots of commentaries, lots of books about the Bible, but how about the Bible itself? I am not against commentaries. I am not against these books. I publish them too. But there is a temptation because these books—these commentaries—are predigested food. Therefore, it's easy to accept the word of God as it is almost like solid food. You don't have to learn how to digest it. And I understand that. That's why you go through these books instead of *the* book, the Bible. If you can only do one or the other I would rather see you not reading these books. If for this reason my publisher is put out of business—I would thank God for it, because it is not a business—it is a ministry. If that meant instead you read the word of God, thank God.

We need to know the word of God, apply ourselves to it, and store it richly in our hearts. We cannot just know it mentally, but we need to really touch it. As we touch the word of God, we touch the Living Word. We touch Christ. We must read it in that way. If there is a rich deposit of the word of God within you, then the Holy Spirit has an instrument in us that He can use for His work. The word of God is called the sword of the Spirit (Hebrews 4:12; Ephesians 6:17). The word of God is like a sword. It cuts like a two-edged sword. It penetrates. It divides. It divides the soul and the spirit. But who is the one who wields it—who uses the sword? The Holy Spirit. He will use His word and touch people. He does this, not you and me. Today we sometimes wrongfully use the word of God to cut people up. Not only in preaching, but in praying too. But if we touch the word of God in the living way, then we allow the Holy Spirit to use the word of God to touch people's conscience. So, I think this is evident. We don't need to labor over it. Those who minister the word need to know the word. They need to really read the word of God.

3—The Minister Needs Revelation

The third need for those who minister the word is for current revelation in the word. When we say revelation, we do not mean that one needs to receive some extra revelation beyond the Scripture. No. Some have proclaimed that they received a new revelation that cannot be found in the word of God. That's heresy. That needs to be rejected. All the revelations of God—all that God wants to reveal about His own Son and His beloved church—are here in this book, the Bible. There are no extra revelations. The "faith once delivered" (Jude 1:3) was completed at the end of the first century as it was delivered to the saints. But it does not mean that today, we do not need revelation.

The apostle Paul prayed for the saints in Ephesus, that God would give them the spirit of wisdom and revelation to the full knowledge of God (Ephesians 1:17). We need revelation. What is it? It simply means this: the word of God is breathed anew by the Holy Spirit. God breathed in the past and the words came forth. The result of His first breathing is the word we have in our hands. This is the eternal truth. It never changes. As we approach the Scriptures these words are at first mere letters to us. But when we read them with the humble spirit, looking to the Spirit of God to interpret them to us, the Holy Spirit breathes again upon the word. Suddenly those words became alive to us personally. They touch our hearts. They become real to us. The words are now personal and no longer that which was written thousands of years ago, but a word spoken today.

With revelation the word is not something spoken in general, but a word for you personally. We call it *rhema*, which is one of the Greek terms used for word in the Bible. The current, living word—*rhema*—is based off of the original spoken word—*logos*. The Lord said, "My words are life and spirit" (John 6:63). The word used there is *rhema*. "The *rhema*-word that I'm speaking to you now is spirit and life." When you receive that *rhema*, that revelation, it becomes life to you and spirit to you. That is what you need. And only with this *rhema* are you able to help people into God's word.

So, those who minister the word of God need to ask the Lord to give them the spirit of wisdom and revelation. That's what they need.

4—The Minister Needs Experience

The fourth need for the ministry of the word is experience. To minister the word of God is not the same as lecturing or expounding on a subject. The ministry of God's word is imparting life. It is imparting Christ. Therefore, you need experience. You need to experience Christ. And that's the reason why those who minister are put into so many circumstances. It is a strange phenomenon. Those whom God wants to use to minister His word, He will put in unique circumstances. The minister himself really does not need to be placed in such environments so often; but God puts him there in order that he may learn Christ and have more experience of Him. After he experiences Christ, he will be able to administer more of Christ to other people.

David is a typical example. God put David into so many various situations in order that he may learn God. And out of his learning, he wrote the Psalms. People love Psalms. Why? Because they are life experiences. They're real. So, brothers and sisters, in ministering the word of God, we need experience.

It is true that sometimes God allows us to speak beyond our experience—to stretch us. But speaking with experience is different—it is much different.

Well, the question remains. If the ministry of God's word is so difficult, who would dare to do it? Who has enough confidence? No one. Usually, people who dare are people who should not. People who cite their incompetency and yet they are constrained by the love of Christ, they simply must minister the word. They have to suffer for it. The standard is high. God never lowers His standard, because the word of God is God himself. It is by His words that His work is done. Therefore, He would never lower His standard.

To minister the word of God universally and to minister the word of God locally are no different. But thank God the Scriptures say, "As many therefore as are perfect, let us be thus minded; and if ye are any otherwise minded, this also God shall reveal to you. But whereto we have attained, let us walk in the same steps" (Philippians 3:15-16). So, even though we are not able to enter into this ministry like Paul or even like Timothy, but let us walk step by step in this. Whatever God has already led us into just do it in your measure. Don't do it beyond your measure. But as you are faithful in your small measure God will increase that measure.

This is why we say it seems as if ministering the word of God universally always begins with ministering the word of God locally. Maybe in the beginning it is just at a time of Bible study or fellowship time. Maybe the Lord gives something of His word and you use one or two minutes to share what the Lord has given to you. And gradually you discover that you are able to minister the word of God in a small group for 5 minutes or even extend to 10 minutes. And maybe, gradually, you'll find that the Lord begins to increase your measure. You eventually are able to minister to the people whom you are with. Maybe there are 30 or 100 gathering with you. And maybe you are eventually able to share with them for one hour or half an hour and people are really helped. The anointing of the Lord is with you and you are gradually developed, step-by-step, step-by-step. So, do not be discouraged. But the standard cannot be lowered. Our mind has to be set on the standard that God has set. And only by this are we able to grow. Just like Paul told Timothy, "Occupy yourself with it that people may see how you make progress in it." (see I Timothy 4:15).

So, brothers and sisters, take heart. In your local assemblies, if you really love the Lord and love His church, you want to see His church built. Apply yourself to the word of God. And if the Lord begins to open up something to you, share it with your brothers and sisters. And at the same time be humble enough to be corrected. Or even to be discouraged. If it doesn't help people, then it needs to be discouraged a little bit. But don't be discouraged at the very beginning. Try again and after several tries then it becomes clearer. May the Lord raise up, in local assemblies where you are, some who are really able to minister the word of God in a way that will build up the church. And that is, I believe what the Lord desires from us.

TITLES AVAILABLE
from Christian Fellowship Publishers

By Watchman Nee

Aids to "Revelation"	The Life That Wins
Amazing Grace	The Lord My Portion
Back to the Cross	The Messenger of the Cross
A Balanced Christian Life	The Ministry of God's Word
The Better Covenant	My Spiritual Journey
The Body of Christ: A Reality	The Mystery of Creation
The Character of God's Workman	Powerful According to God
Christ the Sum of All Spiritual Things	Practical Issues of This Life
The Church and the Work – 3 Vols	The Prayer Ministry of the Church
The Church in the Eternal Purpose of God	The Release of the Spirit
"Come, Lord Jesus"	Revive Thy Work
The Communion of the Holy Spirit	The Salvation of the Soul
The Finest of the Wheat – Vol. 1	The Secret of Christian Living
The Finest of the Wheat – Vol. 2	Serve in Spirit
From Faith to Faith	The Spirit of Judgment
From Glory to Glory	The Spirit of the Gospel
Full of Grace and Truth – Vol. 1	The Spirit of Wisdom and Revelation
Full of Grace and Truth – Vol. 2	Spiritual Authority
Gleanings in the Fields of Boaz	Spiritual Discernment
The Glory of His Life	Spiritual Exercise
God's Plan and the Overcomers	Spiritual Knowledge
God's Work	The Spiritual Man
Gospel Dialogue	Spiritual Reality or Obsession
Grace Abounding	Take Heed
Grace for Grace	The Testimony of God
Heart to Heart Talks	The Universal Priesthood of Believers
Interpreting Matthew	Whom Shall I Send?
Journeying towards the Spiritual	The Word of the Cross
The King and the Kingdom of Heaven	Worship God
The Latent Power of the Soul	Ye Search the Scriptures
Let Us Pray	

The Basic Lesson Series
Vol. 1 - A Living Sacrifice
Vol. 2 - The Good Confession
Vol. 3 - Assembling Together
Vol. 4 - Not I, But Christ
Vol. 5 - Do All to the Glory of God
Vol. 6 - Love One Another

ORDER FROM: 11515 Allecingie Parkway Richmond, VA 23235
www.c-f-p.com

TITLES AVAILABLE
from Christian Fellowship Publishers

By Stephen Kaung

Abiding in God
Acts
"But We See Jesus"—*the Life of the Lord Jesus*
Discipled to Christ—*As Seen in the Life of Simon Peter*
Elijah and Elisha—*One Prophetic Ministry*
God's Purpose for the Family
Government and Ministry in the Local Church
The Gymnasium of Christ
Isaiah
In the Footsteps of Christ
The Key to "Revelation" – Vol. 1
The Key to "Revelation" – Vol. 2
The Master's Training
Ministering the Word of God
Moses, the Servant of God
Nehemiah
New Covenant Living & Ministry
Now We See the Church—*the Life of the Church, the Body of Christ*
Proverbs
Shepherding
The Songs of Degrees—*Meditations on Fifteen Psalms*
The Sons of Korah
The Splendor of His Ways—*Seeing the Lord's End in Job*
Titus
Worship

The "God Has Spoken" Series
Seeing Christ in the Old Testament, Part One
Seeing Christ in the Old Testament, Part Two
Seeing Christ in the New Testament

ORDER FROM: 11515 Allecingie Parkway Richmond, VA 23235
www.c-f-p.com

www.ingramcontent.com/pod-product-compliance
Lightning Source LLC
Chambersburg PA
CBHW060155050426
42446CB00013B/2829